LEADING WITH COMPASSION

Cultivating Connection from the Inside Out

CURATED BY CHANGING WORK

AIMEE SERENE   ISABELLA CHENG   KERRI JACOBS

NICHOLAS WHITAKER   BENJAMIN OLSEN

SARAH ARIAUDO   RACHEL RADWAY

CHIRONA ROSE SILVERSTEIN   SHELLY DHAMIJA

CHRIS L. JOHNSON   QUENTIN FINNEY

ORLANDO WHITE   JOCHEN RAYSZ   EREM LATIF

KARIN FROSIO   MEENU DATTA   VINCENT SMITH

ASHANTI BRANCH   WAINWRIGHT YU   AARON FROMM

JASPAL BAJWA   SCOTT GAUVIN   SABRINA RILEY

BLAIR MORRIS   LORNA HAGEN   SCOTT SHUTE

LEADING WITH COMPASSION: CULTIVATING CONNECTION FROM THE INSIDE OUT

© 2025 Changing Work

Editor: Lisa Thomas-Tench

Copy Editor: Joshua Humphreys

Layout: Natalie Lapre

Print ISBN: 979-8-9911984-2-4

Ebook ISBN: 979-8-9911984-3-1

Contents

The Power in Empathy

The Purpose in Witnessing

The Strength in Conscious Awareness

Foreword

Derek Lewis

Just before I graduated high school, my mom helped me apply for a job at a state residential school and hospital operated by the District of Columbia for children and adults with intellectual disabilities.

I didn't really know much about the place or what kind of job I'd be doing, but I knew that a bus that would pick me up on 8th and H Street every day at 730 in the morning, and drop me off at 4:30. That meant that I had plenty of time to get on the basketball court when I got home in the evenings.

I was one of four student interns. While the other three students worked in the administration building pushing paper or behind the scenes in the canteen, my job was to assist the nurses. I watched them feeding the residents, bathing them, cuddling and comforting and talking to them. It was our role to make sense of what the residents needed. We had to sense these needs by listening to what the residents said, which wasn't always clear. The first few days I was there, they didn't talk to me at all. I had to learn their varied ways of communicating. I had to show up. I had to remember people's names in order to get them to trust me.

Whatever the nurses, the doctors, the staff asked me to do, I did it. I cleaned that place before I left every day. I took pride in my work. I watched the staff at Haven do the same job day in and day out, knowing that they stayed longer and worked harder than me. I was just there for the summer; everyone else was there for life. By the end of my first month, I would springboard out of my bed to get on the bus to support the residents because it mattered to me that I was part of that team, part of that community.

Working at the residential hospital taught me this amazing thing about the importance of compassion and taking care of people, even people I didn't know. I learned that intense feeling of intrinsic reward from doing something that mattered to others, a feeling that continued throughout my whole career.

As I moved into the C-suite ranks and eventually became the first President, Multicultural Business and Equity Development at PepsiCo North America, I worked to raise the bar for everyone around me. I made sure that I was committed to holding the door open for the next generation of leaders to walk through. Holding the value of compassion at work as sacred meant that everyone had the support they needed to level up.

While compassion matters the most to people who are in crisis, to people who don't know where to turn, it also matters in normal situations. Keeping our humanity in mind is just as critical when we're out buying groceries as when we're selling products. Everyone is going through something.

We all have everyday moments where we have choices to make. We notice them all the time when we're up against it, when we're faced with frustration behind the wheel, when our children or parents or partners remind us of our flaws, when we listen to our work colleagues take a tone with us. In those moments, we have to decide whether we lean into old fears, or whether we can summon our better selves, our compassionate selves.

Each of us has the ability to make someone else's life better.

And if *you know* that you have the ability to make someone else's life better, then you need to *go do that.*

Derek Lewis, former president, PepsiCo, is the author of *Survive and Advance*, a memoir about his journey from a challenging childhood in Washington, D.C. during the 1970s, where he protected himself and his younger brothers from the impacts of single parenthood, mental health, and addiction issues, to achieving unparalleled corporate success and becoming a national catalyst for gender and racial equity. Follow Derek at realdereklewis.com and @realdereklewis.

A Letter from Aimee

Self-compassion brought me to Changing Work. I wanted to reimagine a better world of work for myself. Compassion for others brought me to join Scott Shute and Nicholas Whitaker on the journey of bringing the vision of Changing Work to life, first as a volunteer—now as a co-founder. If I could help bring something like this to life, maybe it would help one person not feel the way I did for nearly half of my professional career.

In March of 2023 I got one of Scott's infamous emails. It started with, "I hope this finds you smiling." That in and of itself made me smile.

Perhaps it was the word—because when you say it… you smile.

Or perhaps it was because I had spent the evening prior in deep meditation, my eyes swollen with tears, my heart heavy with the burdens many of us face in the modern workplace—a place that often feels more like a battlefield than a space for growth.

I began that meditation with an exhale—one of those exhales that just screams, "I'm fucking done," as a wave of defeat drew me closer to the ground. I may have even laid down.

I surrendered for a moment.

I set two intentions for what I wanted to call into my life next, because crying every evening in the shower after work wasn't sustainable.

I asked for two things.

I prayed for two things.

I mentally vision-boarded the shit out of two things.

Same same but different in how we go about it.

Let me find people who accept me as I am—who see my strengths and support my growth.

Let me create something meaningful, something that aligns with my values, my purpose, and my passion—my ikigai.

The next line in Scott's email had three important words that tickled my sense:

Compassion + Conscious + Business

My journey with Changing Work is deeply intertwined with a profound sense of compassion, both for myself and for others. This compassion has been a powerful guiding force in my life, leading me through an intense process of self-awareness, healing, and transformation.

Emerging from a long period of introspection, I found a renewed purpose and a calling to effect meaningful change in the world of work. When I joined Scott and Nicholas it felt like an extension of my personal evolution—my integration.

Together, along with a growing community of change agents, we are committed to fostering authentic connections and creating workplaces that prioritize consciousness and compassion. This journey has taught me that compassion is not just an emotion, but a catalyst for personal and collective transformation. It has the power to reshape our environments, uplift communities, and inspire genuine change. It proves that true leadership and meaningful impact begin from the inside out.

Fast forward to today and as you hold this book in your hands you are about to embark on an extraordinary journey with twenty-five remarkable authors. These individuals, each a beacon of transformation in their own right, have chosen to share their deeply personal stories of seeing—truly seeing—others.

This collection is a testament to the collective power of compassion in leadership and the profound belief that true connection begins from within. Each chapter offers a unique perspective on how embracing self-awareness and compassion has transformed these leaders' engagement with the world and the people around them.

The authors in this book, like myself, have navigated the intricate paths of self-discovery and emerged with a renewed ability to connect deeply with others. Their stories reveal moments of vulnerability and growth, where they may have stumbled and even fallen at times. Yet through these challenges they have learned to communicate with authenticity, they have leaned into their journeys, and discovered the profound strength that comes from understanding themselves.

These extraordinary humans have dedicated themselves to fostering environments where compassion and integrity thrive. They exemplify how conscious leadership can transform not only workplaces but also lives, creating ripples of positive change that extend far beyond themselves.

As you delve into these pages, may you find inspiration and encouragement to embrace your own journey of compassion and connection. May these stories remind you that even in our most vulnerable moments we are never truly alone. There is a community of like-hearted people, each striving to make the world a better place through compassion, integrity, and authentic connection.

In community,
Aimee Serene
Co-founder, Changing Work

The Courage in Compassion

Our task must be to free ourselves from our optical delusion of consciousness by widening our circle of compassion to embrace all living creatures and the whole of nature in its beauty. [1]

Albert Einstein

ONE

Insert Coin and Press Start

Isabella Cheng

"Good morning!"
I greeted my coworkers as I entered the office and navigated my way to my seat. It was one of those boring open-floor plans with fluorescent lighting. To make the space more interesting we decorated the walls with colorful video-game art posters, including a few from our project. The desks and chairs were arranged in circles based on teams, making it easy to swivel around for impromptu discussions.

After putting my stuff down at my seat I casually headed to the kitchen to make my usual cup of tea and have watercooler chats with colleagues. Anyone could spark a conversation with the go-to topic: "It's so hot today!" or "It's raining again!" When you've lived in Vancouver long enough you pick up this classic conversation starter: talking about the weather.

I must say, as an introvert, it's a good tip for socializing. At least it gave me something to talk about. Over time I became more comfortable with chatting and learned to ask a few questions to get to know my coworkers better. But I always stuck to my principle of not asking too many personal ones. I didn't want anyone to feel like I was invading their privacy.

I looked at the clock and it was almost 10 a.m. Time to start my day.

"I love this job!"

I had just started at this video game company a few months ago. It wasn't my first game job but I was still early in my career. I was excited about having some flexibility in work hours, the free coffee and tea, t-shirts and jeans as the common attire. And of course, making video games with a group of talented and passionate people.

WORKING in the video game industry has been my dream since I was a kid growing up in Taiwan. On the day before my eighteenth birthday, I flew to Vancouver with my mother and younger brother to pursue a new life. I was hopeful that I could turn my dream into reality.

The style of education I received before adulthood wasn't one that encouraged asking questions in class. Outside the classroom, my surroundings and my (analog) social network taught me that being quiet was a virtue, especially for girls. I was also taught that it was impolite to ask too many questions when chatting with others because it might come across as an interrogation.

At first I wasn't sure how many questions were considered *too many*, and what kinds might be *impolite*. But thanks to my observation and listening skills, I quickly found out that personal questions were often "the issue." In terms of quantity and frequency, asking a couple of *lightly* personal questions seemed acceptable—but not every time, especially if you saw the person daily.

Without fully realizing it, I concluded that the more privacy I gave people the better. And having a clear separation between work and life felt professional and respectful.

Since then, respecting privacy has become one of my core principles. And I carried it with me as I entered the workplace.

. . .

BACK AT MY DESK, I followed my established work routine like a well-rehearsed pianist performing with muscle memory, moving with the rhythm. I opened and cleared my inbox (yes, I'm one of those who prefer a clean inbox) and went through task-tracking and scheduling documents. I made sure every assignee had what they needed to do their job, had reasonable workloads, and had opportunities for professional development.

I genuinely cared about the people I worked with, whether they were internal employees or independent external remote workers around the world. I encouraged them to speak up about their concerns by actively listening, showing appreciation, and making them feel heard and valued. I tried my best to accommodate different time zones, availabilities, communication styles, and turnaround times for submitting work and responding to emails. I also had contingency plans in case someone needed to take sick days. My thorough documentation allowed me to quickly identify potential risks so that I could respond quickly and ensure the project stayed on track.

I was on top of it. Everything was running smoothly and we were ahead of schedule. Everyone was happy. Until I opened that one email. It came from the other side of the world.

"...he passed away..."

Those were not the only words in the email, but they were the only words I could remember.

As I read the email my eyes widened and stayed wide open. I couldn't blink. My whole body tensed up and couldn't move. I wasn't wearing headphones, yet I couldn't hear any typing sounds or mouse clicks, nor the conversations of my teammates nearby. All the ambient office sounds were suddenly muted. It felt as if I were the only person in the world, frozen in time, while everyone else around me continued their activities. The only thing I could feel and hear was my own heavy heartbeat.

"Maybe I read it wrong."

I spent the next few minutes re-reading that sentence, over and over again, trying to convince myself that I had misunderstood. But those words stayed the same—cold, hard, timestamped. I finally accepted what I had read. He had taken time off. Permanently. From our world.

I couldn't comprehend it. How could this happen to someone I worked with almost daily? Just a few days earlier I was still exchanging emails with him about his task. Everything was fine. When the planned submission date arrived, I didn't see his email in my inbox.

"That's a bit odd," I thought. He had been very responsive and punctual with his previous submissions. In fact he was one of our most reliable external workers on this project, so I trusted he would send it soon. We were ahead of the overall project schedule so we still had time.

A day passed, and I decided to check in, but no response. Another day went by, and still nothing. We were running out of time, and there was no way to check on him through colleagues—he worked independently.

Little did we know, another one of our external remote workers happened to be a friend of his. It was she who sent the email.

THE IDEA that any one of us could disappear at any moment was not something that came across my mind at work. After all, my career had just taken off and the game industry was supposed to be that fun, happy, "dream" industry, as some people called it. I was naive. I was so focused on work that I forgot we are all human beings.

I thought I was prepared to face any project risks, but nothing could have prepared me for this. What made it worse was that I didn't even know what he looked like, since all our communications were through email. Realizing this, a sense of guilt and shame rushed through me.

It took me a while to gather enough courage to deliver the news to my team. Everyone was just as shocked as I was. The air in the office was filled with sorrow. I signaled permission to take it easy for the day. It was the right time to make space for people to process their emotions, including myself. It was the right time for self-compassion.

In the years that followed more tragic news came. Someone I worked with in person and had become friends with. The loved ones of coworkers.

Although it sounds basic, the realization that work and life are just two sides of the same coin transformed how I lead. I learned that caring for my teams doesn't just mean managing workloads, supporting their growth, or asking a couple of lightly personal questions now and then. It needs to be deeper, more human.

But what exactly does it mean to be "more human"?

Nurture. As I started to create more space for vulnerable conversations, deeper connections were formed. Over time, I discovered more about the different types of challenges people endure, often hidden behind their professional masks—challenges that aren't often talked about at work or widely understood by the general public. But they impact lives deeply—how people work, communicate, behave, and live.

Some struggle to focus in an open office. Others find social interactions extremely challenging. Some work better when they can rotate between different tasks throughout the day, others are more productive by sticking to one task for an extended period. There are also those who are slow readers and thinkers, needing more time to process information before they can effectively participate in discussions (oh hey, that's me!).

Creating an environment where people can thrive not only helps them reach their full potential but also increases the productivity of the team and the organization. To achieve this we must listen to understand what people need. By continuously showing genuine care through active listening and patience, we can create a safe space for them to open up and reveal their real challenges. They might share the reasons behind these challenges, or they might not —and that's when we need to respect their privacy.

Detect. When you really get to know your team's personalities and work styles, you'll spot those subtle S.O.S. signals much easier.

One day, a newly promoted manager requested a quick one-on-

one meeting with me to discuss some project matters. As soon as he joined, I had a feeling this meeting was going to turn into something else, and I was right. He showed signs of relief when he saw me and said, "Today is crazy! So many meetings!" with an exhausted smile. I had worked with him long enough to sense he wanted to chat more, so I decided to use the time to let him speak his mind.

He shared many of the common challenges that new managers face. I listened carefully and asked questions to better understand the context. Then I took the time to guide him through those challenges, one by one. The meeting turned into a coaching session. By the end he walked away feeling more motivated and we also managed to cover the original topic, which only took a few minutes. Although the meeting ended up longer than scheduled, the benefits were long-lasting.

By the way, I was not his supervisor. I was just helping out.

Evolve. Certain types of challenges are harder to identify and address because they've been ingrained in the workplace and human culture for so long. These are the deep roots—our beliefs, values, and unconscious biases, to name a few.

These often require more than just surface-level changes. They involve raising awareness and challenging our assumptions, beliefs, behaviors, and norms.

Let's reflect: during the hiring process, do you or other interviewers tend to believe that candidates who display strong confidence, or who chat with you like old friends, are more competent, or a better "cultural fit", than those who are quieter? Have you ever thought that a woman looks too young or too old for the job? Do you believe that extroverts make better leaders than introverts?

By learning about these topics, we can confront uncomfortable truths and foster a more equitable and inclusive workplace. However, lasting change requires more than awareness. It requires us to grow and adapt beyond our ingrained beliefs. In doing so, we'll be able to harness untapped talents and achieve collective success.

Amplify. Small gestures of kindness and care can make a world of difference. This is why, in recent years, I've started sharing my experiences and extending my support beyond a single workplace, reaching new graduates, aspiring professionals, communities, and non-profit organizations. Often when we lift others up we find that we rise too. That's how we strengthen each other.

Let's bring the human element back to work and care for people beyond their tasks and titles. Create time and space for genuine conversations. Don't let people suffer in silence. Helping others ultimately helps you and your team.

When we treat each other as human beings and foster deeper connections, we become more resilient during tough times—at work or in life. This is the true power of communities.

Life isn't a single-player game, nor is it linear. And we don't have to fight alone.

The game has already started. How will you play?

Isabella Cheng

ISABELLA CHENG is a project and product manager turned talent and organizational development coach across various industries. She believes that small gestures of support can shift a person's career and life trajectory for the better. With a mission to reduce the gap between rich and poor, Isabella extends her reach beyond borders and welcomes opportunities to collaborate with diverse organizations while striving to empower as many people as possible.

TWO

The How-Not-To-Fake-Compassion Playbook for Leaders

Kerri Jacobs

This room is a virtual one (we are midway through the COVID pandemic lockdown) with fifty faces in boxes on my laptop screen. I welcome the group of senior executives to the Leading with Empathy workshop, the three-hundredth I've delivered since creating the program for leaders to promote compassion and understanding in the workplace. The shift from in-person to online has actually helped my attendees show up with more vulnerability (it's harder to be full of bravado when you have a cat purring at your ankles or a toddler asleep in the next room), and the pandemic experience has made even the most skeptical leaders more aware of the need to foster belonging in their teams in order to be successful. When you strip away the ego boost of striding through the office as the boss, even the most self-regarding leaders realize the fear tactics they've come to rely on don't work like they once did.

In the virtual room we are midway through my workshop and I'm seeing for the three-hundredth time (sending waves of warm validation through me) the scales fall from the eyes as these leaders start to understand how they can avoid causing suffering in the workplace. Then one attendee unmutes himself to ask me a question.

"It feels like you're giving us tips and tricks on how to lead with kindness, but isn't that dangerous? Aren't you just showing toxic managers how to pretend to be compassionate? Isn't faking compassion even worse than not having any in the first place?"

His question brings my whole being to a juddering stop.

Have I created a how-to-fake-compassion playbook for toxic leaders?

If the actions I'm coaching these leaders to demonstrate aren't truly authentic are they doing more harm than good? The faces in the boxes lean closer to their cameras, intently awaiting my response. Their attendance is mandated at this training so I know not everyone has shown up with positive intent. But those are typically the leaders who need to hear the content the most.

I'm viscerally triggered by the word 'pretend', which is what led to the breakdown and subsequent career change that brought me to this work. Showing up every day as a leader who acts the way leaders in tech were expected to; suppressing my emotions and natural instincts; being a version of myself my family wouldn't recognize as I pretended to be someone I wasn't.

And in doing so, making myself very, very, sick.

I'M THINKING BACK to a very different room. It's three years before I was asked the question about pretending. This room has seventeen chairs arranged around the four walls. The one I'm sitting on is directly opposite a TV mounted high above a 'No Cell Phone Use, Thank You' sign. It's showing back-to-back episodes of a home improvement show where in each installment the homeowners react to a kitchen transformation with the kind of uncontained joy I haven't felt for a very long time. Whoever took away the remote control muted the sound before they did so and didn't activate closed captions. But even as a novice lip reader I can clearly make out the *oh-my-god*s that each homeowner repeatedly exclaims when the makeover is revealed.

Oh my god indeed. The other sixteen chairs are empty. I've been alone in this silent room for six or seven episodes now, ignoring the cell phone warning sign as I frantically google my symptoms and doom scroll through what could be wrong with me. As my phone battery dies so does any semblance of me keeping myself together. I look at picture after picture on my camera roll of my beautiful family, their faces wobbly because I'm now both sobbing and shaking.

Here's one of my husband and daughter hugging when reunited after a trip.

Here's my son grinning as he holds the Nerf gun that I was so conflicted about Santa bringing him.

Here's me onstage in corporate-leader mode, espousing the value of female leadership to the next generation of managers.

I add a new picture to the roll as I capture this hospital waiting room to remind me of the lowest point in my life. I'm waiting for another set of results, this time from a doctor, not a search engine. I'm praying these results will explain why I'm feeling like my life (which from the outside looks rosy: happy marriage, healthy kids, successful career in Big Tech) is not worth living.

I know all about burn-out. I've read multiple articles (well, headlines and opening paragraphs, who has time to read whole articles?) and I've nodded gravely when learning that a colleague has had to take leave (which was becoming a regular occurrence)— so I know it can manifest in my body both mentally and physically, as the incoming test results will unmistakably attest. As the next new kitchen (*oh my god*) is revealed, I experience a profound stomach-dropping realization that years of stress, overwork, unrealistic personal expectations and toxic leadership have finally taken their toll. I can't keep pretending. Something has to change.

At my lowest moment clarity emerged and maybe I even uttered my very own *oh my god*. I could not and would not continue for a minute longer in the role I'd played for two decades as a successful sales leader in corporate America. Instead I'd use my position and experience to lean full-bodied into the leadership trait I was best known for, the one I sometimes felt embarrassed to be defined by, and which ironically was also the one often weaponized against me ("too soft", "not cut-throat enough")—compassion. My health diagnosis was predictable and devastating (severe depression paired with digestive breakdown) and I became the next colleague to be discussed with grave nods. With the great privilege of medical leave and health insurance, I took a leave of absence and set up my out-of-office reply. In the months that followed I not only got better and stronger physically and mentally, I also resolved to dedicate myself to ensuring fewer employees end up desperate and broken in hospital waiting rooms.

The workplace should never be a place of suffering. And if you think a good salary, benefits, and the envied status of working for a highly regarded company negates suffering, think again. Suffering doesn't discriminate, and the guilt of feeling that your pain isn't valid because of your privileged circumstances—the notion that you should be grateful and indebted to a corporate employer—compounds the misery and leads to suffering in silence.

The antidote to suffering is compassion. Compassion is the feeling that arises when you are confronted with another's suffering and feel motivated to relieve it. If I ask you to think about the best leader you've ever worked for, I know you'll think of the one who cared about you the most. And I know that that leader likely helped you do the work you're most proud of.

The expansive body of research on workplace compassion shows time and time again that how your employee feels drives how they perform. Compassionate leadership leads to higher employee retention rates (especially among historically excluded groups), increased creativity, higher productivity, and ultimately better business results.

Knowing the disproportionate impact managers have on the employee experience, I focused on that group. Anticipating that a program centered on empathy and compassion in leadership might be a hard sell to senior executives ("the last thing I need is to be told to be nice"), I centered my work on data. I shared studies that correlate a happy workforce with bottom line improvements, and paid attention to the sunk cost of not leading with compassion—losing your best people, knowledge lost in transition, overstretched teams bridging the gap left by departing employees, becoming a less attractive destination for future top talent. With the support of my compassionate and visionary VP, my return to work was in my new role as a teacher of compassionate and empathetic leadership.

When after my breakdown I started to prioritize my physical and mental health, I realized that I could read about the root causes, learn holistically about healthier living and study the benefits of a balanced lifestyle. But years of productivity propaganda programming, multitasking and attention-span-zapping TikTok-brain meant I was more receptive to specific instructions—a to-do list of recovery, if you will. Therapy, sleep, meditation, improved diet, increased activity and social connection were too vague for me. I needed to drill down further to specific actions, often very small, that had an impact. I learned very quickly that my empathy workshop attendees (senior executives, with busyness badges of honor and limited time to focus) also responded more positively when given specific compassionate behaviors to adopt.

For example, a general discussion on the benefits of gratitude was one approach, but when translated into a direct action item I noticed attendees scribbling it down furiously. Asking them to prioritize being actively present in one-to-one meetings felt too fuzzy a request. But reframing that as a direct ask to consciously make your hands visible (and thereby demonstrating that you have their whole attention) made it more specific and tangible.

This 'give me specifics' approach widened as I carried out research on the leadership behaviors which people experienced that made them feel included or excluded. Working with focus groups I gathered an initial list of these behaviors, then surveyed over 3,000 individual contributors—asking them to rank them or tell me what we'd missed. Regardless of nationality, gender, tenure, location, role, department, age, or level, the results were always the same: the leadership behaviors that had the biggest impact on employees feeling included, and therefore made them likely to stay with the company and over-perform, were not associated with promotions, salary raises, or high-profile projects. They were human behaviors, like managers remembering personal details about their teams, showing genuine concern when their report shares something they're going through, being visibly supportive of extra-curriculars, being an ally, sharing their mistakes, and being consistent.

When it came to exclusionary behaviors the biggest response was around managers having 'favorites'. Interestingly this wasn't related to who gets promoted, it was about treating people (albeit unintentionally) differently in the human moments like celebrating milestones or friending someone on social media. The data overwhelmingly showed that simple things like not providing a quick explanation when moving or canceling meetings, or sending contextless 'you there?' messages, were eroding trust and building fear. But the good news was that each of these examples could easily be altered with tiny behavioral changes. A Compassionate Leader to-do list, if you will.

So here I am in the virtual room with fifty senior executive faces in boxes on my laptop screen.

In one box is the familiar face of a very senior executive to whom I once reported. This man had made fun of an LGBTQ+ colleague's queerness over drinks with his management team and talked about another female colleague's "resting bitch face." He knew I was a proud feminist and enjoyed needling me by initiating conversations about why women should dress in a feminine way to win bigger deals, or by asking his leaders to rank people by their "hotness." If I rose to his bait, which I tried not to do, and called out his misogyny or homophobia, he'd lean back with a satisfied smirk and say, "Here she comes, the fun police." His behavior was waved away as "a bloke having a laugh", and because he was also charming and good at other aspects of his job he rose triumphantly through the ranks—leaving damaged but too-afraid-to-speak up employees in his wake, me among them. I am quite sure if the workshop invite had been optional he wouldn't be here today and I'm already extremely unnerved by his presence. Then the question of whether my work is making it easier for toxic managers to feign compassion is asked: *Have I created a how-to-fake-compassion playbook for toxic leaders?*

I hear my daughter laughing in the next room as her online school day comes to an end. I feel my cat rubbing against my ankles. The faces in the boxes wobble and I take a deep breath.

"If you are responsible for causing someone's suffering, you have no business being in a management role. If you see someone in your workplace suffering, and you don't feel compelled to act to ease that suffering, you have no business being a leader. If you fake compassion to wield power over someone and advance your own agenda, you have no business leading people. I am assuming positive intent when I share this guidance, and if your intent doesn't match that, you have my permission to exit the call now."

None of the boxes disappear but my heart is racing and I start to wonder how I'll explain to my husband how I lost my job by giving a group of VPs my unfiltered perspective. The silence is broken swiftly.

"*Oh my god*, Kerri," says an unmuted face, the most senior on the call and in the organization. "Dropping the truth bombs on us at 3 p.m. on a Tuesday!"

I swallow hard and will myself not to cry. But he has more to say.

"I want everyone on this call to take her words to heart, because our workplace must never be a place of suffering, and if I ever learn that your actions have caused pain or you've deliberately avoided easing pain, you have, as Kerri said, no business being on my leadership team."

And in that moment I experience pure kitchen-makeover-level joy.

Kerri Jacobs

KERRI JACOBS has worked for some great compassionate leaders and some who miss the mark. Her obsession with empathy in leadership inspired her to create the Leading with Empathy program for leaders at Google and beyond. A Scot based in the US, she used to read books, watch films, and see a lot of Broadway shows, but these days mainly doom scrolls on social media, doodles, and comfort eats.

THREE

Baggage Unpacked

Nicholas Whitaker

I 'm lying on a bathroom floor 7,500 miles and three flights away from home, in a foreign country where I do not speak the language, and I'm convinced that I'm having a heart attack.

I'm several days into another multi-week business trip that has taken me to places like Indonesia, Malaysia, Vietnam, Thailand, and now Hong Kong. In forty-eight hours I'll land in California for a team event before a few days of camping with my partner—a brief respite before another leg through newsrooms in Eastern Europe and the Middle East.

This has become my new normal: weeks on the road with only a few days in between to reset. Airport, taxi, hotel, conference room, client meal, taxi, hotel, repeat. I wake up in the mornings, unsure of what city I'm in. At each hotel room door I fumble with the multiple keycards I've collected in my pockets from two countries ago.

I've been going nonstop since my last presentation to hundreds of journalists at a national newsroom. I can't even recall which country I just left. The event was a blur; I was already feeling off. Somehow I got through the day, blaming exhaustion and jet lag— but as I land in Hong Kong it's getting worse and the feeling terrifies me. *Gotta shake this off, and get home, Nick.*

I desperately need sleep, but tonight my nervous system has other plans.

I am in a cheap airport hotel, lying on the hard bathroom tile, trying to catch my breath and calm my racing heart with breathing exercises and guided meditations I've found online. The coolness of the tile helps; it has calmed me down before when this has happened. But this time it's worse, and a deep, unshakable fear grips me.

I'm drenched in sweat, soaking through my socks and boxers. The rest of my business attire is scattered around the darkened room, discarded as I stumbled in intending to take a shower. The floor was as far as I got. There's a tightness in my chest, my heart pounding so hard I feel it in my ears. My hands tremble, and dizziness swirls in my head. Is this really happening? Am I dying here, alone on the floor?

Time has passed. Or has it? It's hard to tell. The numbers on my watch taunt me, blinking 2 a.m. but I can't be sure it's right—I don't remember resetting my watch like I usually do. Normally I set it to my next destination to adjust for jet lag, but this layover is short and time loses meaning in these liminal spaces of airport terminals, hotels, and conference rooms.

My heartbeat reverberates throughout my body, too fast and irregular. Something is very wrong. Hard dread settles in my stomach and I feel nauseous. My mind is scattered across time zones. I feel like I've left parts of myself behind, like missing luggage in... where was it? Kuala Lumpur? Ho Chi Minh City? No, Bangkok.

It's still dark out. *Just a few more hours until your flight,* I tell myself. *Walk it off and get home, Nick. You're better than this.* But doubt creeps in. What if I'm not?

There's no lost and found for what's left behind by this relentless pace. No way to let go of the baggage I've picked up along the way. Not with the skills I have at that moment.

Days before, political protests in Bangkok forced us to evacuate our Toyota van and escape on motorcycle taxis for a harrowing ride through gridlocked traffic to reach the safety our hotel. It rattled me.

The irony wasn't lost on me. As a motorcyclist, the ride should have been thrilling but fear overshadowed any sense of adventure. Later that day a grenade went off outside our hotel, killing a woman and a child and injuring dozens.

My work-travel colleagues and I will eventually trade jokes about close calls like this with a kind of gallows humor you only pick up after the fourth or fifth time something like it happens. After a while this all becomes normal workday stuff.

Is it Wednesday? Thursday? It's hard to keep track. I just follow the travel plan crafted weeks before: flight numbers, hotels, meeting times—all formatted for easy recall on a phone with poor Wi-Fi.

But nothing prepared me for this. Lying on the bathroom floor, I realize something is very wrong. How do you say, "I'm scared and need help," in Chinese? How do you say it in English as a young man in America?

My work as an international trainer and representative of my company takes me to newsrooms worldwide, helping journalists adapt to the changing digital landscape. It's important work, or so I tell myself, but at what cost? The relentless travel, the pressure, the isolation, the chaos—it's eroding me from the inside out. I'm not adapting well. I'm still blaming myself at this point. This is just bad nerves or weakness. Shouldn't I be able to will or logic my way out of this?

After frantic internet searching I conclude I'm not dying, I'm *just* having a panic attack. Eventually I'm able to pick myself up, body aching and exhausted, and take a cold shower. The icy water stings but grounds me as I sit shaking on the shower floor. Soon autopilot kicks in. I'm able to get dressed and head to the airport. *Just keep moving, Nick. Man up and get home.* Years later I'll learn concepts like self-compassion and positive self-talk, but for now the best I can do is will myself into action. My internal dialogue, the one that sounds a lot like my father, is one of sticks, not carrots—and definitely not one of kindness. It works, but in time I'll learn that it comes at a cost.

Hours later I'm sipping bitter airport coffee, hands trembling, watching as my plane, my escape route home to safety, pulls in. I should feel relieved, but there's just numbness and fear. I'm still years away from a mental collapse but I know something has cracked inside, and I have no idea how to fix it. Not yet. Those cracks just get bigger over time, like a neglected rock chip in a windshield, spidering across my field of view and blurring everything.

This wasn't the first sign that I needed help, nor the last, but it still takes me a long time to act. Eventually the fear of losing my job and the realization of the harm I was causing my partner and colleagues by not dealing with it finally forced me to act.

I was accumulating shameful behaviors but still only realizing it after the fact, and then punishing myself for it. Reactive emails, snapping at managers, arguments with my partner. At one offsite I felt rage creeping up my spine. I find myself pounding a table with my fists, triggered by a leader's comment that they were "disappointed in us" despite our obvious hard work. I heard someone righteously shouting, "This is a failure of leadership!" and as I looked around the conference room to see who it was, my eyes blurry with tears and rage, I realized people looked uncomfortable and were avoiding eye contact—with me? Wait, was that me shouting? Am I the bad guy here?

A few weeks later, during yet another argument with my partner, she left the kitchen abruptly, flooded and overwhelmed by my spiraling tirade over… I can't even remember now. I lost it, punched a cabinet door so hard that blinding pain shot up my arm and into my neck as I collapsed on the floor, sobbing uncontrollably. Years later, two fingers on that hand still aren't right. I sometimes lose my grip, whatever's in my hand dropping to the ground as a reverberating reminder of the damage I've caused, and how much I've healed. But in this moment, as I'm again crumpled on a floor, all I know is I'm out of control, my hand hurts, and I don't know why.

A few days later, I'll start weekly therapy and learn words like dysregulation and dissociation. My years of struggle begin to make more sense and I'm grateful I've found help before it's too late. I lost two friends to suicide and there were times during my journey that I wasn't far behind them. One missed connection away from self-annihilation.

A saying that I now use with clients—"Where else does this show up in your life?"—was a new concept for me then. It was something I picked up from my therapist and soon I was noticing patterns at work and home. Regular meditation practice and journaling helped me cultivate the necessary awareness, along with lots of cognitive behavioral therapy. Eye movement desensitization and reprocessing helped with my startle response and reactivity. But it was the intentional self-compassion practice that allowed me to forgive myself when I struggled— self-compassion for the past harms I inflicted on others and for the deep shame, guilt, and self-loathing that I for so long carried silently. It gave me a more loving way to talk to myself and helped me understand the physical and emotional deregulation that my complex trauma had imposed, something I had experienced for decades without knowing it. This wasn't my fault. I'm not a bad person, I'm just wounded. I can recover from this.

Later, at a team offsite, I shared part of my story during a team-building exercise. I assumed mine would be the worst. I was stunned at the vulnerability of others, especially the leaders. Hearing their stories made me realize I'm not alone at all. We all carry baggage; some carry-on size, some to be checked at the ticket counter, wrapped in security plastic and marked "fragile" in big red letters—but we all have baggage.

Over rooftop drinks and pizza one summer day in NYC, a manager shared their own story of panic attacks during work trips and how it almost destroyed their career. If they could share in that way and not only increase my trust in them but give me hope, what might happen if I shared my story with others too?

Soon I was finding opportunities to host workshops on mental health awareness, mindfulness, and compassionate communication for teams across the company. I was invited to speak at larger events, becoming an unofficial advocate for mental health and mindfulness in my corner of the company. I hosted mental health discussions where colleagues shared their challenges in small groups. We listened without giving advice, validated each other's experience just by holding space.

I now volunteer more for our workplace mindfulness programs and continue to deepen my own practice and training. Along the way I've discovered the widespread need for this work. Where I once felt isolated, I now realize many colleagues also suffer in silence. They approach me after sessions, sharing their experiences, thanking me for speaking up. They DM me during town hall meetings to thank me for using my voice to advocate for change. Everywhere, people grapple with stress and burnout, often unnoticed beneath professional facades. I know all too well the loneliness this causes.

Something compels me to give back, to share, and to help others find new ways of relating to their own their challenges. In part, what drives me is gratitude. I'm just happy to be alive. Perhaps I'm also making amends for the harm I've inflicted on myself and others.

But it all feels like plugging holes in a leaking dam. Most programs at work support individuals but don't address systemic issues causing poor mental health outcomes. High-pressure environments glorify overwork, fostering a hustle culture where burnout is encouraged. The drive for scale at all costs has a cost, and employees pay the price. Band-Aids won't stop the hemorrhaging these conditions cause. True change requires a shift in organizational culture.

I've learned that compassion starts with understanding our own struggles, and extends to recognizing the silent battles that others may face—even those of our leaders and colleagues who may behave in harmful ways. They too are likely wounded and need not only the necessary training to help them be excellent leaders, but also the language and techniques to help them heal before they inflict their wounds onto others. They too need our compassion.

Compassion has been the bridge connecting my suffering to purpose. By opening my heart, even to those who have caused me distress, I found a path to healing and connection.

We have a responsibility to each other to do our own inner work and hold each other in compassion. I'm trying to do my part.

Through mindfulness facilitation, coaching, and community building I'm now helping others navigate their own journeys, just as I continue to navigate mine. But collective action is essential for lasting change. This awareness led me to co-found ChangingWork.org, a community dedicated to transforming workplaces from the inside out. We focus on building self-awareness and compassion, fostering conscious leadership and business practices, and addressing systemic issues that contribute to disengagement and poor performance and well-being.

By fostering open conversation about our struggles and supporting one another through them, we can create more compassionate workplaces. Collectively we can move from cultures of competition and isolation to ones of collaboration and mutual support, benefiting shareholders and stakeholders alike. Together we can challenge the systems that perpetuate unhealthy work cultures. We can advocate for workplaces that prioritize mental health and well-being, ensuring no one has to suffer in silence. We all deserve that much.

Nicholas Whitaker

NICHOLAS WHITAKER is the co-founder of Changing Work, a coach for high performers, a conscious leadership advocate, a husband and a cat dad. With decades of experience in tech, media academia, and entrepreneurship —along with deep training as a coach and mindfulness facilitator—Nicholas empowers clients to reconnect with themselves and the world around them in order to lead with authenticity, self-awareness, and compassion.

FOUR

The Heart of Responsible Innovation

Benjamin Olsen

I was a maestro for the day. A few stories up, in the middle of pre-pandemic Manhattan, I was interviewing the world's leading experts at Microsoft for a new course on a nascent field called Responsible Artificial Intelligence. I recorded one visionary after the next, a full studio experience—cameras, lights, and all—with windows pointing out to the city's skyline.

While filming and between sessions, I imagined how my work would set the stage for new possibilities to bring ancient philosophical wisdom—ethics, questions on how we should live—into the world of technology. I was building the first-ever learning experience of its kind. I questioned my new friends with as much artistry and care as I could, and they shared their wisdom on central words—called principles—that would guide the growth of its practice: fairness, privacy and security, transparency, accountability, reliability and safety, inclusiveness. Behind the camera I was safe and in control. I was empathetic and calm, holding space for what was unfolding.

As the day rolled by, a new thought kept coming back to me: *There's time—should I get in front of the camera? What would I say once I got there?* I jotted down a few points on a sticky note and sat in the chair to start filming.

What came to me was a surprise, as if the idea had always been there: *we must grow alongside these machines we create.*

I knew that I was boldly jumping into a conversation that was going to transform responsible technology innovation at Microsoft and throughout the industry. What I could not have known then was that these words also became a prophecy for the kind of transformation I myself would need to undergo to become a responsible technology leader. But before that would happen, I had to take another jump—and fall in the process.

The course, in the meantime, became a success, along with a public access version that has now educated tens of thousands worldwide. Internally at Microsoft, it became the first required course of its kind for all employees—hundreds of thousands were engaging with my work. I was promoted then offered a full-time role in one of the main responsible artificial intelligence teams. At the same time I became enamored with a vision of what my true purpose there could be: coordinating all learning, education, and evangelism as a leader of a new organization which the multiple AI teams would look to for direction, coordination, and synthesis. So with the vision held close, I declined the offered role and made the pitch for the team's creation.

"You're no longer part of the inner circle."

The words of the executive as they turned down my pitch were painful. It was so clear to me that the team and role were needed. Not only was my vision left without a path forward but the door of the previous offer had closed too. Those whom I served every day were no longer accessible to me in the same way. While this was happening, the pandemic started to bring everything to a standstill and the sudden isolation I was feeling was echoing through the entire world.

Without a way forward at Microsoft, I answered the call of a friend who was charged with building a responsible innovation team at Meta. He was creating a more holistic foundation to shape products and experiences and wanted me to lead education and evangelism. My days of isolation opened up to a new adventure, mediated through virtual calls and virtual colleagues and the pandemic rhythm of hunkered down work and family life. With the new rhythm I turned to old practices that had served me in the past.

I sat in meditation before and after virtual work, struck yoga poses to process the day, breathed in the silence of the forest, and an inner landscape both familiar and wonderful unfolded. At that point cobwebs surrounded my experiences with church and formal religious practice. At one point I had left college with a one-way ticket to Rome, debating whether to embark on a life of poverty, contemplation, and celibate service to God and neighbor. In the hush of those days I felt that I was missing something in the daily grind, even though I was making a good living and shaping a new field. But I was many things before I was a technology professional, and I needed to heal the rift between my spirit and my work. I had to go deeper.

On the wintry saltwater shore of Puget Sound, I plunged into a weeklong silent retreat. The only connection to others was through Zoom calls led by mindful movement experts, mindfulness and compassion teachers, and other retreatants. I would wake up to waves crashing outside the sliding glass doors that led straight into the tiny hut of a house, stir a bit of mushroom coffee, and turn on my computer for lessons and practice. Qigong opened my body and mind, then slow solo walks on the nearby beach. Picking up pebbles, putting them back down again (though I did keep a few). My presence and sense of time expanded. And I began to turn over like wave-worn pebbles ancient phrases in my mind. Blessings, prayers for my family, for my work community, for the world:

"May you love the love that loves you."

"May you be held by the one who holds you."

"May your joy be with you always."

"May you be at peace."

The limitlessness of the space inside! Flashes of intensity and feeling combined with my experiences of God in childhood, of my sense of the Divine in my dreams, the tears I shed in college looking for answers to life, my destructive draw to pleasures, my aversion to the pains of adult responsibilities—all coalescing into the present. In my journal I wrote: "This week, I've spent most of my waking hours drinking in love from the sea air, the place I've known as home. Hundreds of locks have been opened. I am called by this love to be a healer in the world." I am one who blesses, one who holds my heart open to the endless horizons of words like joy, love, peace—becoming these words, not just saying them. At the very core of me are these words, dancing with power and with fire.

Equipped with my newfound inner transformation, I was asked to return to the responsible artificial intelligence team in the Windows organization at Microsoft. The words and values guiding my practice—fairness, transparency, accountability, privacy and security, reliability and safety, inclusiveness—had not changed. And yet within me I knew the secret reality-changing power of a word truly known.

One of these words I seek to truly know in my work is fairness. Systems should allow for the fair and equal treatment of all who use them. We all understand this viscerally: "It isn't fair" is an often-repeated mantra of children everywhere. And yet, sit with the term long enough and it kaleidoscopes. Fair comes from Old English, and in addition to its normal definition is associated with beauty and with festivals. Is fairness a perfectly balanced scale, two sides staring each other down, or is it a destination wedding?

Yes, it's necessary to code for balancing an indeterminate system's outcomes towards equity. Reduction of fairness to a practice whereby we measure and quantify it and call it "fair" is common enough with artificial intelligence. But as the practice matures, the kaleidoscope of fairness—the wild landscape of its more ancient meaning—surfaces in people's expectations of what the system should do for them. At its best the word "fairness" pulls a bright and festive future into the present, and responsible innovation is starting to notice. Checking quantified fairness boxes as they are today misses intangibles that practitioners would catch if they held on to an open and almost limitless version of fairness. They would turn the pebbles of their work over and over to look at the user experience, solicit customer experience at every turn, and create a constantly learning and evolving system which they would craft with the care of an artisan, the leader of a new guild.

EACH DAY, as I venture out into wave after wave of new advances in technology, I don't just work with words in code. Words make up systems which are themselves increasingly capable of gaining momentum from data's training wheels and generating new wonders. The people I work with use systems to make more systems. And in the context of business, we do it so we can serve customers, capital, growth, efficiency. More insidious words and experiences are also there: pain, suffering, harm—things we seek to avoid or eliminate by weaving better words carefully into our systems. Words become the prayers, the blessings—sometimes the curses—of technologists and their technologies.

The right words, with the right understanding and the right care, form a buoyant, glory-filled raiment—a vestment that compels us rise above the waves of difficulties and complexities in our work and lives. We can wrap not only ourselves, but those who are suffering, those in pain, in the same robe of love and kindness that originates from an abiding openness to the surprise and splendor of words.

Who do you serve? I ask myself every day.

Some days the answer springs forth as a word: "love," "justice," "peace."

Others, it echoes in the chambers of my heart as, "The One who is love, here and now." Not an abstract concept, but a presence, there with me through the incense of liturgy in worship. It's also burning inside me while I sit in a conference room, turning a new model or an artificial-intelligence experience over like beach pebbles until I see into the horizon of possibilities—praying the good into the fabric of the systems, casting out the evil as best I can with the power of this loving presence.

. . .

Recently, driving back on the freeway from work to home, I asked what love wants and I heard back: "To be One." Not in any specific place or time, but everywhere present, in all times, in all things, to be One.

The privilege of responsible innovation is to be one small part of the symphony of Oneness. The heart of responsible innovation is no less than our God-filled hearts growing alongside the machines and creations that we're inspired to make. Let us bless these machines—and each other—as we pick up the pebbles of our daily work, shaping them into the tools and experiences of the future. And let us all discover the hidden heights and depths of responsibility in the loving words we speak into being.

Benjamin Olsen

BENJAMIN OLSEN is a technology executive and a pioneer in trustworthy innovation for planet-scale platforms and experiences. He also guides individuals and organizations through the inner transformation that is needed when creating systems that truly help us flourish. He co-authored the first responsible artificial intelligence standard at Microsoft, led responsible innovation education at Meta, and has contributed to industry-wide collaboration through IEEE and the World Economic Forum.

FIVE

Humanizing the Workplace

Sarah Ariaudo

As I sat in my new office sunlight streamed through the window, bouncing off the cars in the parking lot and casting blinding glints from windshields. I gazed out, lost in thought, remembering Beth and her words—the ones she shared on one of our last days together. Beth had been the Cancer Center Director for thirty-five years, caring for the people, navigating the complexities of multi-location clinics, the varying departmental systems, and managing the processes of their private radiation therapy practices. When I arrived she had just two weeks left before retirement, and in that brief time she became more than a guide: she became a voice of wisdom I didn't know I needed. As we walked across the parking lot from one center to the other, our conversations flowed from work to family, from goals to the intricacies of life.

Her words were measured, deliberate. "If I can give you any advice," she said, her voice carrying a quiet weight, "don't make the same mistake I did."

She told me about how her daughters said she wasn't there for them. As a single mom she worked so much to provide for them, but they don't remember the money.

"They remember that I wasn't there."

Despite the sun warming our bodies, I felt a chill. Her words spoke to my heart. I remember the way my throat tightened as I listened. Damn. I wasn't ready for it but I was glad she shared. As an overachiever and workaholic, obsessed with perfection, Beth's advice spoke to me. It was a message to my soul. She was right. I had just returned to work after taking a year-long break to focus on my newborn daughter. My ambition, my drive to succeed, had always been a double-edged sword—pushing me forward but pulling me away from the things that mattered most. In Beth's words I saw my future, and I knew I had to keep my values and priorities clear and at the forefront.

The two weeks we spent together before she left were short, but her impact lingered. Her advice settled in my chest like a stone, heavy but grounding, reminding me to check in with myself regularly, to make sure I wasn't getting lost in the hustle. Now, 45 days into what I once considered my dream job, I felt the weight of those words as I prepared to make this place my own. I had the incredible opportunity to not only ensure our clinics provided exceptional care but also to shift our focus from merely technical excellence to true holistic well-being. I wanted to create an environment where every person—employee, patient, or visitor—felt seen, heard, and cared for.

But as it often happens life had other plans for me and soon my leadership would be put to the test. It was a typical afternoon, the hum of the clinic fading as the end of the day approached. My team was wrapping up their tasks when the lead physician called an impromptu staff meeting. She had pulled me aside earlier to share the news. Thirty-five of us crammed into the cold, sterile space of the CT Simulation room, the faint hum of machinery filling the silence as we waited for her to speak.

Beth had passed away.

Immediately I stepped into action. I turned to my team, giving them space to process the news. I quickly assessed who could continue working and who needed time. Then I spoke to the patients in the waiting room, ensuring them we would be providing their treatment in a timely fashion while apologizing for the slight delay. As the clinic day came to a close I checked in with each team member, making sure they felt supported.

I had always prided myself on being calm under pressure, quick on my feet, ready to handle anything that came my way. It was almost second nature—ignore my own needs, suppress my emotions, throw myself into the troubles of others. It wasn't just that I enjoyed helping people—it was more like an addiction. A distraction. Helping others kept me from facing the darkness inside myself. The messiness. The fear.

Professionally I quickly climbed the corporate ladder, always taking on more than one job, volunteering for extra shifts, spearheading projects—anything to keep the inner voice quiet. The more I worked the worthier I felt. And if I kept moving fast enough I never had to sit still long enough to confront my own feelings. Cancer patients were the perfect outlet for my obsession—people enduring immense pain, both physical and emotional. I could help them, immerse myself in their suffering, and detach from my own.

But this strategy—this relentless distraction—came at a cost. Eventually it caught up with me. My body, worn down by years of ignoring my needs, began to rebel. I got sick. The kind of sickness that forces you to re-evaluate everything. At the time, I was in my mid-twenties and should've been thriving, but I was constantly tired, plagued by digestive issues, skin breakouts, unexplained weight gain. I looked like I had it all together but inside I was falling apart. People even told me they envied how "easy" I made life seem. If only they knew.

I pushed myself to keep going until I couldn't anymore. That's when I found yoga. At first I hated it. The slow pace, the silly words—but it was all my body could handle. Then one day something clicked. In the middle of class I closed my eyes and felt a strange, almost magical, freedom. It was as if I was floating outside of myself, watching my body move without pain, without stress. For the first time I felt free. Free from expectations, from my own relentless drive. I wanted more of that feeling, so I signed up for yoga teacher training—not because I wanted to teach, but because I needed to learn how to keep that feeling alive.

The training became my sanctuary. Five hours every Friday night and full weekends of practice, all while working full-time and traveling. It didn't add to my exhaustion—it saved me from it. For the first time in my life I was learning to listen to my body and give it what it needed. I was 28 years old, and I had just begun the process of truly caring for myself.

As I began my journey of healing, it wasn't just my body that changed—my approach to leadership evolved too. I started paying attention to the unspoken needs of my team. I tuned into their emotions, their body language, their silences. I began leading with intuition, compassion, and pushing back against the old *this is how it's always been done* mindset. I trusted my instincts, and as a result my teams thrived.

When I took over for Beth to manage these cancer centers I remembered her warning about not letting work take over your life. People have lives outside of work and as hard as we may try, our personal lives impact everything we do. I wanted to know my team —not just as employees but as people. I met with each of them individually and asked two simple questions:

1. Why did you choose this career path?
2. What lights you up outside of work?

Their answers told me more than I ever could have imagined. Brian, who was studying to become a pilot, was sharp, technically savvy, and always willing to take on extra work. Liz, a dedicated mom, was nurturing and flexible, always ready to support her teammates. Julie, who loved scrapbooking, was a natural leader— organized, detail-oriented, passionate about taking on new projects. These conversations laid the foundation for the strong, compassionate team we were building together.

The days following the news of Beth's passing were heavy. Grief hung in the air, thick and palpable, but I knew my role was to guide my team through it, not away from it. I called in our Employee Assistance Program to provide support and offered my office as a private space for counseling. I didn't micromanage—I trusted my team to take care of themselves, each other, and our patients. And they did. Something beautiful began to unfold in those weeks. The team drew closer, became more open, more connected. We weren't just a group of people working together anymore—we had become a community.

I wasn't expecting recognition, but it came. One day, a team member pulled me aside and thanked me for creating space for them to grieve. Another, one of our lead physicians, approached me with quiet praise for how I had handled the situation. Her words meant more than I could express, but to me it felt like the only way forward—to care for the people around me, to lead with compassion. Isn't that what leadership is supposed to be?

Not everyone shared that view. My boss, stationed 30 minutes away at the main campus, arrived for her monthly visit just after the dust had settled. As I updated her on Beth's passing and how the team was managing, her expression hardened.

"You're encouraging them to bring their problems to work," she said bluntly. "No more therapy sessions. They have work to do."

I looked at her, letting her words settle between us for a moment before I responded.

"People don't leave their problems at home," I said gently but firmly. "They carry them with them—whether we choose to acknowledge it or not. Giving my team the space to process their grief means they'll be more present, more focused, and ultimately more productive."

She didn't flinch. Her gaze was unmoved by my explanation. There was a long silence, the kind that feels like a test of wills. It was clear she wasn't swayed and in that moment I realized I was facing a much bigger challenge than I anticipated.

I knew my boss wasn't someone who was going to shift her mindset overnight. She was deeply entrenched in her ways—metrics, outputs, deadlines. In her eyes, feelings were distractions, something to be dealt with on personal time, not during office hours. But I had no intention of backing down from the approach I knew worked.

She wasn't convinced. But in that moment, I realized I had a choice: conform to the old way of doing things or continue to lead with compassion. The decision was clear.

Managing up with someone who saw the world so differently meant I had to be strategic. I had to approach her the same way I'd want my team to approach me—with empathy but also with a firm grounding in facts. I wasn't going to win her over with emotions alone. So I took a deep breath and laid the groundwork for how I would move forward.

First I reframed the conversation in terms she could understand—productivity, efficiency, and the bottom line. I didn't talk about grief or compassion directly; instead I spoke her language. I let her know that I'd seen a direct improvement in the team's performance after giving them the space to regroup, making sure to emphasize the tangible results. I highlighted that our patient satisfaction scores were up and morale was noticeably better. I made sure she saw the connection between giving people room to process and their ability to produce results.

Professionally managing up wasn't about challenging her; it meant proving that a different way of working could yield better results. She wasn't one to be swayed by emotions or team dynamics. To her, success was measured in dollars and deadlines. I made sure that each interaction spoke to those concerns while subtly reinforcing that the changes we were making weren't just benefiting morale—they were driving the business forward.

When we reviewed the clinic's performance I didn't just focus on the numbers, I highlighted team engagement, the improving patient outcomes, and increasing productivity. By digging into our workflows I saw an opportunity to improve a key process: our billing.

After implementing new processes, we were able to capture additional revenue each month.

It wasn't just about the extra revenue or the improved metrics, it was part of a broader picture of what was possible when the team was fully engaged and empowered. It was about creating a space where people could do their best work, and in doing so, improve every aspect of the clinic's operation. The results spoke for themselves—$30,000 in additional monthly revenue, higher engagement, and a thriving team. This approach worked because it wasn't about choosing between people or performance—it was about realizing they were always connected.

But this journey wasn't just about managing up—it was also about managing myself. I had to remind myself that not every battle needs to be fought out in the open. Sometimes the most effective leadership happens behind the scenes, through quiet persistence and carefully chosen actions. It was about finding the balance between standing my ground on the things that mattered and finding common ground where I could.

Months later, when the results of the yearly engagement survey came in, the numbers told the story I already knew: employee engagement and satisfaction had increased by over 26%. These weren't just statistics. They were the evidence of a team that felt valued, supported, and cared for. My quarterly metrics consistently met or exceeded expectations, validating my belief that leading with compassion isn't just a feel-good strategy—it's essential to success.

But this journey was more than a leadership lesson; it was deeply personal. It started with me acknowledging my own humanity, recognizing my imperfections, and learning to sit with the discomfort of stillness. It was through that self-reflection that I learned to truly listen—first to myself, then to others.

As leaders we often focus on the bottom line, on metrics and goals, but the real success comes when we acknowledge the human factor. Leading with compassion doesn't just improve engagement—it empowers teams, fosters connection, and builds a culture where everyone can thrive. It's not about numbers on a page. It's about the lives we touch along the way.

And in the end, those lives—and the way we lead them—are what matter most.

Sarah Ariaudo

SARAH ARIAUDO, an executive health and wellness expert, partners with organizations—including those in pharma, healthcare, and technology—to transform team engagement and performance through well-being and strengths-based leadership. With over 15 years of leadership experience and certifications in positive psychology, coaching, and mindfulness, Sarah takes a tailored approach to aligning individual and team strengths and by integrating tools like Human Design and Strengths assessments. She empowers leaders to build resilient, connected, and high-performing teams.

SIX

The World We All Design

Rachel Radway

T ear a sheet of paper into eight smaller pieces. On each one write the name of a person or animal you love or an item that has special meaning for you, whether it's sentimental, symbolic or practical—choose eight of the people or things that are most important to you in the world. Take a moment to reflect on the choices you made, on what each one means to you. When you're ready, turn all eight pieces of paper over so you can't see what's written on them, shuffle them around, and spread them out in front of you.

Now, imagine that civil war has broken out in your country and there's fighting everywhere. Homes, schools, hospitals, shops, offices —everything's being destroyed and there's nowhere safe to go. You and your family make the difficult decision to leave the country and seek asylum. It will be a long and dangerous journey. You can take only what you can carry. You set out together, praying you'll all make it safely to your destination, where you'll have to start a new life—find a new home, jobs, schools, maybe even in a new language.

You make slow progress while trying to keep away from any fighting. After several hours of rough travel, an insurgent attack suddenly blocks your escape route. You're eventually able to get away, but it's cost you. Choose one piece of paper at random. Look at it to see who or what you've lost. Crumple up the piece of paper and toss it far away.

You travel for days, sleeping only when you can find shelter. An abandoned shack seems safe for a few hours of rest, until a massive storm floods it and damages most of what you've brought with you. Choose three pieces of paper at random. Look at them to see who or what you've lost. Crumple them up and toss them away.

You continue your journey for weeks, facing one obstacle after another, until you arrive at your destination with nothing but the clothes you're wearing and the person or item written on your last piece of paper. You've lost everything else.

It was the summer of 2018 and I was attending a weeks-long program on intercultural communication. This exercise, led by an instructor in an intensive workshop, was much longer—more detailed and more complicated than what I've just described. Halfway through I was in tears, grieving the inconceivable losses that weren't even mine; crying over the state of the world and the tens of millions of refugees facing these kinds of experiences, and much worse, for real—wanting to help however I could. This was just one of a series of powerful workshops and courses I took at the institute and it made a permanent impression on me.

Two years later, at a training for hospice volunteers, an instructor asked us to tear up a sheet of paper and start writing down the names of people we loved and things that held value for us—including our physical senses of hearing, sight, and smell. She took us through the same exercise I'd gone through during the intercultural training, this version designed to help us understand the experience of a terminally ill hospice patient rather than a refugee. Knowing how it would go, steeling myself for all the loss, didn't make anything easier. I cried and cried. I wanted to do whatever I could to take away the patients' pain and suffering.

It surprised me that I was affected so strongly by something I hadn't actually experienced, but it shouldn't have: I've always been highly sensitive—to everything, including energies and others' emotions. I cry for, and laugh with, well-drawn fictional characters and can put myself in someone else's real-life shoes. I often feel what they're feeling, whether I've been in a similar situation or not. Compassion, though—going beyond empathy and understanding and taking action to ease the suffering of others—especially people I didn't know personally—came less naturally to me.

I GREW up in a family of smart people with high standards and expectations. I was an early reader. I have few fond memories of my father, an attorney who specialized in doing business in Latin America, but we shared a love of words and languages, and he regularly quizzed me on Spanish vocabulary and English spelling. I distinctly remember being confronted at eight or nine years old by "antidisestablishmentarianism." My mother was also an attorney, then left corporate law to join the executive team of a national non-profit. She was a single mom working long hours at a stressful job, commuting between the Bronx and Manhattan, and coming home to two kids who weren't particularly easy. She was strong and competent and did the best she could for all of us. There was definitely some stoicism in there, on both parents' sides. Strength, competence, and independence were messages I took to heart. But compassion isn't something I remember from my childhood.

I was just trying to find my own way. We'd lived in three other states before landing in New York, just before my eighth birthday. I'd picked up a suburban Ohio accent in the few years we'd lived there, which didn't help me fit in with the second-graders in New York. The city kids weren't very welcoming and I missed the friends I'd left behind, so I kept to myself a lot. I wore skirts every day when most kids wore jeans and I brought craft projects to work on during lunch break so I'd have something to do while the other kids played with each other. I was awkward. I guess it wasn't that surprising that I was assigned to the third-grade class with the "troubled" kids; the teachers and administrators probably had no idea what to make of me.

Eventually I made a few new friends and I did well academically. Then I got into a school for gifted kids that started in seventh grade and had to leave my friends behind, again. In this new school everyone was a little different; I was no longer the odd one out. I loved learning, had some wonderful teachers, and was challenged in good ways. I made a few new friends and hung out on the fringes of various groups of kids.

There were still cliques and bullies though, and I still didn't fit in. In seventh grade I was targeted by a mean girl who'd been in the elementary school that fed into our combination middle/high school. She and her entourage taunted me, called me names, damaged my things. I finally went to the school guidance counselor for help and while the bullying eased a little, it didn't stop completely. At the end of the school year the mean girl left, and without their leader's prodding the others were less interested in me.

In eighth grade another tormentor appeared—and he'd been watching me for a while. The year before, in a Communications & Theater class, my best friend, two boys and I had put on an adaptation of *Arsenic and Old Lace* that the teacher loved—so much so that she had us perform it for other seventh-, eighth- and tenth-grade classes. We had fun with it and were even invited to audition for one of the drama groups. But a student who'd seen us perform latched onto us and built an entire imaginary planet around us in his head. I was the president, my best friend the VP, and the role of our other friends was unclear. Something to do with the country of Bhutan—again, unclear. It may sound like harmless imaginative fun, especially since it came out of an acting class assignment, but it was more than that. The student—who was brilliant but deeply disturbed—harassed us endlessly. At one point he provoked my usually even-tempered friend into punching and shoving him into the hallway lockers. He left at the end of that school year and I learned later that he had paranoid schizophrenia.

All this happened not long after a few traumatic incidents at home involving a housekeeper hired to keep my brother and me out of trouble after school. She also turned out to have paranoid schizophrenia and had been institutionalized off and on, a fact she was supposed to have disclosed to my mother and hadn't.

As if we weren't already questioning and confused enough at that age, I spent my early teens wondering how and why I attracted this kind of energy and attention. And subconsciously I built a little bit more of a buffer zone around myself. Distance was defense.

In my twenties I met a psychic in San Francisco who taught me how to protect myself from the unwanted energies and attention I'd continued to attract. But the defensive walls I built then were a little too solid; they didn't let much in at all.

For years I focused on my career and didn't really have a social life. I'd found my way into tech and I just worked. Until 2014, when I was a director at a Fortune 500, leading a global team of ten, and realized I could no longer function the way I had been. I was so burned out that I ended up quitting my job, selling my home, and moving to rural Peru, then Ecuador, for the time and space I needed to start to recover.

Living in a small village in the Ecuadorian Andes with an international population that included many healers and energy workers, I focused on healing myself and started breaking down those walls. The deconstruction and healing continued in northern Portugal, where I lived for another year and a half, then in Oregon when I returned to the US—six months before attending the Summer Institute for Intercultural Communication workshop that my story opened with.

Around the time of the hospice volunteer training, I returned to the tech world. I was more intentional this time though, and eventually managed to job-craft a role focused on team operations, employee engagement and DEIB (diversity, equity, inclusion, and belonging)—areas I was passionate about and recognized for. When I was affected by the startup's first large layoffs I did something I'd started thinking about years earlier—I got trained and certified as a coach.

. . .

EARLY ON IN building my coaching business I was reminded of all I'd learned about my sensitivities and the gifts and challenges that came with them. I went on a deep dive to learn more. After sharing some of my work I was approached about writing a book. And in that writing process I learned more that's been life-changing.

I'd always known I was wired a little differently. What I didn't know was that in addition to being highly sensitive, I also have ADHD and a bunch of autistic traits. Learning about my own neurodivergence and neurodiversity in general, my whole world shifted. My understanding of myself and others changed. Patterns in my life made sense for the first time. My loud inner critic got a little quieter; I was finally able to give myself some grace.

And I focused my work on supporting others like me—smart, talented high-achievers who somewhere along the way pick up messages that they're crazy or weird or broken or wrong. They're none of these, and I get a lot of joy from witnessing them learning more about their brain's wiring and starting to accept that it's not them. It's the world we didn't design.

They say compassion is both innate and learned. It can also be blocked—by trauma, our environment, and other factors. Like any other emotional muscle, we can exercise it and practice until it becomes natural.

We can remember that we're all dealing with, or have faced in the past—or will face in the future—loss or injustice or devastation of one kind or another. And despite our many differences, we all want to feel safe, connected, loved—that in the most fundamental ways we're more alike than not.

Those two workshops I took years ago gave my compassion muscle a workout it hadn't had in many years, maybe ever. Discovering my mission, helping leaders who are wired differently to create the conditions they need to thrive, ensures that I use it regularly. And when these leaders are truly thriving they're ideally situated to cultivate safer, more inclusive, and more compassionate workplaces everywhere (my not-so-secret secondary mission).

That will be the world we all design.

Rachel Radway

As a certified leadership and executive coach, facilitator, and speaker, **RACHEL RADWAY** helps women who are wired differently get out of their own way and create the conditions they need to thrive. Lessons learned through multiple careers in tech and non-profit—and living in nine countries—shaped the experience, wisdom, and compassion she offers her clients. Rachel's book, *Perceptive*, is due out in summer 2025.

The Grace in Change

Perfection is inhuman. Human beings are not perfect. What evokes our love is the imperfection of the human being. So, when the imperfection of your animus or anima, peeks through, say, This *is a challenge to my compassion.*[1]

Joseph Campbell

SEVEN

Slowing Down and Showing Up

Chirona Rose Silverstein

I 'm walking slowly down a well-worn path in a field of dried-out grass. As I walk I observe the ants slowly building their hill and the intricate designs of the various flowers. I occasionally pick and eat blackberries from the invasive bushes encroaching the paths. I stop and stare at a weathered, naturally shaped wooden sign that reads "Women's Extended Walking Area", painted in dark blue with a lighter blue outline. Similar signs are everywhere I go: Dhamma Hall Women's Entrance, Women's Dining Room, Women's Residence. In the noble silence (no verbal or non-verbal interaction with fellow meditators) of the Vipassana meditation course we have no books, journals, or devices. Signs identifying me as a woman are all I have to read. I begin to attune to how I feel reading the signs and a message becomes crystal clear: I do not identify as a woman.

I had started this ten-day Vipassana course on my thirty-third birthday. Even though I identified as genderqueer by then, I had been socialized and identified as a woman my entire life. About three months before this course I had been interviewed in a publicly posted company blog for pride month about why accurate pronouns are so important. As a genderqueer person using both she and they pronouns, I spoke about the impact of being immersed in a community of queer people. I shared the freedom I felt to try on different pronouns and gender identities the way I might try on different clothes and ask, *How does this feel in my body?*[1]

Since I had started using "they" in addition to "she" as a pronoun, almost everyone I engaged with outside of my small queer community still referred to me as "she." Both in life and at work, leading a global inclusive leadership program at a big tech company, I was frequently included in groups labelled as "women" or "ladies." People quietly ignored the "they." I did not feel seen and deeply longed for someone to acknowledge my genderqueerness by calling me "they." What would it take for me to stop using she? Why did it feel both so necessary and so hard?

GROWING UP, both of my parents struggled with addiction in very high-functional ways—few of their friends, family, or colleagues had any clue and I didn't even find out myself until high school. From a young age I took on as a survival mechanism the harmonizer role in my family. Being a harmonizer created a lot of barriers for me in how I thought about my own identity. When I started attuning to my internal barriers on the Vipassana course, I realized that asking everyone around me to change how they refer to me felt like a heavy social imposition. As someone who tended to put everyone else's needs first, I dedicated most of my time every week to creating an environment that embraces everyone's unique identities. Self-advocacy to get people to accept and embrace *my* unique identity felt much harder.

Vipassana meditation taught me to sit with my physical and emotional discomfort with equanimity, to trust that the discomfort would dissipate. On this course, after many hours of crying and reflection, I had a deeply spiritual moment of feeling acceptance from my father who had passed away six years prior. I felt a physical lightness as I defined my gender as non-binary. I was ready to leave behind the "she" that was no longer part of my identity and to show up more authentically me. I decided there was no rush to come out to everyone immediately and gradually I informed the people around me. I am very fortunate I was surrounded by people who immediately accepted my shifted identity. Unfortunately, getting my pronouns right proved a much bigger challenge, particularly for my colleagues, most of whom also worked in our Global Diversity and Inclusion office.

Over the next year, I spent an immeasurable amount of time and energy giving presentations about pronouns, explaining my gender identity to people I had just met in the inclusion workshops I was facilitating, deciding whether to say something when I was misgendered. It was always easier for me to speak up when someone else was misgendered. I slowly lost trust and distanced myself from my peers while doing my best to advocate for myself and other enby (shorthand for non-binary) employees. On a 2021 Employee Inclusion Survey, those of us who self-identified as non-binary had one of the lowest scores related to visible role models.[2] I felt stuck about where to seek support within the company because my colleagues, my friends, oversaw the LGBTQ+ employee resource group—and I didn't want to out them as poor allies.

In one of the workshops I facilitated, we discussed the idea that you aren't an ally unless someone else calls you an ally, which became more personally resonant. There was one person on my team who was a powerful ally—as a cis straight woman, she was leading the effort to get pronouns on our badges. She put together the pronoun presentation content with my inputs then took over giving those presentations alone when I no longer had the energy to do so. I witnessed her on multiple occasions correct people when they misgendered me.

Outside of work, I was fortunate to spend most of my time in the queer community, where sharing pronouns was a standard part of introductions, where people regularly corrected themselves and each other, and where gender exploration was embraced.

ABOUT A YEAR after this Vipassana course I had a hard conversation with my manager. I informed her I was deeply hurt and disappointed by the constant misgendering by almost everyone on our team. Though they had verbally accepted my identity, they were not doing their internal work to even see themselves misgendering me. To her credit, my manager listened, and allocated time for me to very vulnerably share my experience with our team (something I asked for). She then created a plan for the team to work on their misgendering that required minimal time and energy on my part. I was only asked to give feedback on whether things were improving, which became a regular part of our weekly one-on-one meetings. My manager's plan, which included pairing up teammates to work on their pronoun usage and saving the transcript from our team meetings for pronoun review, did significantly decrease the misgendering. I was already burnt out, and four months later, when I was given the option to take a cushy severance package as part of company-wide layoffs, I knew it was time for me to leave.

I continue to encounter opportunities to shift more deeply into my identity and navigate being an openly non-binary person both with strangers and people I know. Almost two years after leaving my corporate job, I participated in Burning Man for the third time. Burning Man, a yearly late-summer gathering of around 80,000 people who—using a gift economy—build a city in the Nevada desert, is a place that allows me to show up more authentically and explore different aspects of myself. My campmates, many of whom knew me when I was still using "she", were continuously catching themselves misgendering me and profusely apologizing. While this was a significant improvement over my corporate experience, it still required energy from me to hold space for their apologies and I felt exhausted having to do this repeatedly. I wrote a poem to help them understand and shared it in our camp meeting. Here's an excerpt:

Girl, Woman, Lady, Sis
These terms don't fully fit
It's draining to receive constantly
Your challenge around my identity
It limits my ability to be free
What do I need from you?
Figure out what you need to do
Respect my time and capacity

When you think to share your struggle with me.

THROUGH MY GENDER JOURNEY, I experience first-hand the emotional labor of having to explain my identity over and over and I constantly hold space for the apologies and justifications of well-meaning people who struggle with my pronouns and other gendered language. I've learned to advocate and care for myself by politely disengaging in conversations about my identity when I don't have energetic capacity, asking trusted allies to have conversations with people on my behalf and processing my feelings through creative expression, journaling, and community support.

But, what about being on the other side?

As a non-binary person, I often carry the emotional labor of others questioning my gender identity. What is it like for people with other identities—am I embracing their identities and showing up as an ally for them? This experience shed further light on my own journey as a white person that led me to try to show up as an anti-racist ally.

In June of 2020, I participated in a three-day anti-racism intensive for white people called "Seeing the Racial Waters", co-facilitated by Robin DiAngelo and Carlin Quinn through Education for Racial Equity (ERE.) Myself and the forty-four other people in attendance were challenged to notice our physical body responses and our tendencies to move away from emotions towards cognitive processing as we discussed and observed racist concepts and actions. Robin and Carlin held us in loving accountability for our racist perspectives, language, and actions—challenging us to sit with our discomfort. The course did exactly what its title implied—it helped me to see racism everywhere: internally, in individual interactions, and systemically in the world around me. This experience was a shock to my system. I felt an immense amount of grief and sadness that I will carry with me my entire life. I'm grateful that I was awoken to these feelings as they drive my life-long commitment to collective liberation. As a white female-presenting, able-bodied person, I have the privilege of being able to choose when to self-identify as other, which means that I can often opt out of explaining my identity in social situations. Many people cannot easily hide aspects of their identity and I now better understand their experience of being asked to constantly explain their gender, sexuality, race, culture, language, disability, or other aspects of themselves that present different from what is considered normal.

As humans we have deeply wired habit patterns, neural pathways that have been literally worn into our brains. We cannot change our patterns overnight, and we will make mistakes— in fact they are necessary and often lead to the most powerful realizations and shifts.

It's important to get comfortable being uncomfortable. Do the inner work to be aware of what you don't know and what differences are hard for you to understand. Invite yourself into curiosity; seek to understand, but know you don't quite understand, and might never understand. It is impossible to see and catch yourself making mistakes in the moment without cultivated self-awareness—for me this includes daily mindfulness practices and trusted people who can lovingly reflect my behaviors.

Be aware of the difference between intent and impact. Most of the time, we have positive intentions with our words and actions, but they may unintentionally have a harmful impact on others. Do your best to invite feedback and become aware of when your impact did not match your intent, adjusting where possible. Build community with other aspiring allies with whom you can process your mistakes instead of burdening those already impacted.

Always seek consent to repair harm with someone and accept that they might not be open to having that conversation. Never justify your actions to the impacted person with, "That wasn't my intention," or similar language. You may need to accept non-closure with the person you harmed. The most important piece of making amends is doing your own work and showing up differently the next time you are in a similar situation.

When interacting with people who are different from you and seeking to learn about their experiences, make sure to first ask yourself:

- Is this something I could learn/research on my own without burdening this person?
- Do I already have a trusted relationship with them?
- If so, how am I checking in to see if they have capacity/energy/interest in talking to me about this topic?

Doing this hard and often messy work to unlearn and shift how we're showing up expands the breadth and diversity of close, meaningful relationships that we are capable of cultivating and maintaining. I am deeply grateful that my colleagues ultimately leaned into the mess. I remain in contact with many of them as I continue to embrace the mess of my own lifelong unlearning journey.

Let's all aspire to a future in which we are each able to see ourselves, to be with our discomfort, to own the impact of our actions, and to shift our behaviors. We cannot do this alone. We must support each other on our individual, unique journeys to create a world in which everyone is fully embraced for who they are.

Chirona Rose Silverstein

CHIRONA ROSE SILVERSTEIN, they them, is a life transition coach and ritual designer who supports LGBTQIA+ community and allies. They worked for eleven years at Intel, first as an engineer then managing global inclusion programs. Chirona is committed to lifelong learning, working towards collective liberation through education, spiritual practices, and wealth redistribution. They love spending time community-building, singing, and communing with nature with their dog Oz and loved ones.

EIGHT

Use of Self

Shelly Dhamija

I am the third girl who was born out of the desire for a boy.

One day in fifth grade, right after lunch I was late for class, so I ran. As luck would have it a teacher stopped me. She preached on how girls should not be running in corridors. I was already anxious for being late and hearing this made me furious. I did not say anything to her, but the anger lived with me. Every time a teacher would say, "Girls should not do this," or, "It should be boys who do that," it made me angry.

Little did I know then that it was connecting back to the fact my parents wanted a son but they got me. All of these comments made the wound deeper and my need to be needed and loved kept growing with age. The constant reminder that I was born out of the desire for a boy made me feel unwanted and unloved. That need shaped my behaviors: how I approached academics, my relationships, and my career.

I constantly looked for people in my life who would need me, in both my personal and professional lives. I helped people and unknowingly expected certain behaviors from them in return. This vicious cycle continued until, one day, my life turned upside down.

. . .

I MOVED to the US in 2016 and looked forward to finding that happiness I'd been looking for since childhood. Despite my social network I felt alone. All my friends and colleagues were driven by the clock and there was no spontaneity in making plans to hang out. All my interactions were very formal and superficial. This was a huge contrast to how life was back in India, where warmth and intimacy were part of my everyday experience. Even though I had been living by myself for years there, I never felt as lonely as I did in the US.

I put all my energies into my professional life. I kept working harder and harder without any meaningful outcome. On the contrary, I got constant feedback on how to work differently. This feedback wasn't about the content of my work but was directed at my personality and behavior. Loneliness with added triggers kept opening my childhood wounds and I served myself up as a scapegoat for a highly visible program at work. It shattered me to the core.

While I had the courage to face it, at the same time I felt broken and had no desire to live. I went to bed hoping not to wake up the next morning. As I drove to work I wondered if I might have an accident and die on the spot. Constant crying and these negative thoughts kept draining me and one morning I just could not get out of bed. I cried nonstop for hours that morning and as the exhaustion hit me so did the idea of needing professional help. The realization that I needed help somehow made everything feel worse.

It wasn't easy to seek help but I had run out of options. I reached out to Amy, a dear friend who had stood by me through this misery. I shared with her the state that I was in and expressed the desire to get out of this misery as I couldn't take it any longer. She complimented me on the courage it took to acknowledge that I needed help and then acting on it. She introduced me to an amazing therapist and thus began the journey of healing myself. I am grateful for reaching out to Amy for help and not holding myself back. Through therapy I realized that I was very self-aware, but instead of showing kindness and compassion to myself I was unkind and lacked self-compassion. It took me a while to acknowledge the negative view I had of myself.

The insight of awareness isn't enough, I discovered—it's just the starting point. Understanding my behavioral patterns, triggers, and deep wounds had to begin with self-compassion. This involved letting go of judgement and acknowledging that making mistakes is the foundation of learning and growth.

I started treating myself in the way that a kind mother would treat her five-year-old daughter. When a mistake is made, a good mother lovingly tells her daughter that it's okay to make a mistake. She explains to her how not to make that mistake again.

With a firm commitment to practice, I built my emotional muscles. I learned to stop judging myself and I was surprised to see how, in turn, I let go of judgement for others as well.

One day at work, my manager sidelined my perspective in a leadership meeting in a very unconstructive way. It triggered me, and instead of taking a breath, I reacted. As the meeting ended, I got angry at myself for reacting and within a few seconds of being angry I caught myself repeating the pattern of being unkind to myself. I took a deep breath and told myself that my manager was unkind to me and that the situation was a reflection of her personality, not mine. I forgave my manager for her unkindness. I forgave myself for my anger at myself. With kindness, I enabled myself to be in the space between stimulus and response to make the right choice moving forward.

The way I showed up at work and being open to new perspectives led to being accepting of situations and people. This not only improved my skills but also resulted in my colleagues being open to my ideas. I felt included as colleagues asked me for advice and guidance.

My therapist had told me that all the relationships in our life are a reflection of one's own personal relationship with oneself. As I reflect, I truly experienced that transformation. As my relationship with myself healed and seasoned so did my personal and professional relationships. Focusing on self-compassion not only helped me grow but also became an instrument for influencing the growth of people and systems around me.

David Jamieson, Matthew Auron, and David Shechtman define "Use of Self" as the conscious use of our whole being in the intentional execution of our role for effectiveness in any situation.[1] The aim of Use of Self is to be able to execute a role effectively, for others and the system we are in, without personal interference (e.g., bias, blindness, avoidance, and agendas) and with enough consciousness to have clear intentionality and choice. Our Use of Self should always be thought of in a specific context, exercised through some role, in service of something helpful, and aligned with our personal intentions (i.e. our mission, vision, goals, and values). Who we are always goes with us into each of our roles and situations. Our collective knowledge, thoughts, feelings, experiences, and vulnerabilities inform all that we do.

Ironically, learning more about ourselves is not a solo endeavor, as researcher Samuel Culbert once wrote. How we react to a comment from a friend or a colleague or a family member, or even a stranger, tells a great deal about the behavior patterns we have.[2] As we reflect and dig deeper on our reactions, we learn that voids within self are leading us to be triggered. This comes to the surface only when we interact with others. During my Master of Science in Organization Development program, I discovered that my uniqueness made me an outlier. This at times reduced my ideas to being just one person's idea in the room. When consensus is the default decision-making technique, my ideas were dismissed. This triggered lack of being needed and I reacted and this in turn gave me the playground to understand myself better and to work on self.

With continuous practice affirmations such as, "I am kind, compassionate, beautiful, smart and intelligent person," followed with, "I have enough, I am enough, I am supported," helped me heal my emotional wounds. In the process I became compassionate to myself. I became calmer, more confident, comfortable, and relaxed. I became the advocate of my needs, brought clarity to those around me, and navigated situations at work in correct and meaningful directions. This transition from being "needy" to advocating needs in a compassionate way led to my creating space for others to listen and respond effectively.

The most important insight I had through this journey of being self-compassionate was that once the void inside me filled, it helped me be open and present for everyone around me. I am able to feel their emotions and be there for them. Feeling complete in myself helped me be energetic and engaged. Being open and present helped me create the space for everyone to bring their point of view. My focus shifted from how I respond, to being curious about what is driving me, what experiences of mine formed my point of view, what energizes me?

APPRECIATIVE INQUIRY IS one of the ways of starting the journey of compassion. It's a philosophy and practical method for searching for the best in people, their organizations, and the world around them. You start with affirming past and present strengths, then inquire about stories that give you positive energy and what it feels like when you are at your best. You open yourself up to seeing new potentials and possibilities—decide which actions you can take to make those new possibilities a reality.

To take one example, building psychological safety for teams is not about sitting in a circle and sharing praise or brushing over problematic scenarios to help people feel better about themselves. It's about finding a place in which difficult conversations about failure, misjudgments, and left-of-field ideas, become part of the fabric of day-to-day teaming. Many teams in companies are too nice to each other because they don't feel psychologically safe. They don't hold each other accountable, they don't challenge each other or dare to share their wildest dreams about what they might achieve together. Conversations are bland, vanilla, boring, and disastrous. The power of moving from a deficit-based attitude to strengths-based attitude, from a problem-solving mindset to a building-possibility mindset—is empowering.

We have our biases by which we interpret what is happening around us. A way to overcome these is to ask ourselves the questions

—what am I seeing, what are my beliefs, what facts do I have, can I do it in a different way? This line of self-questioning increases awareness, takes away judgement, and leads to being compassionate. This then opens the possibility of being curious about the points of view of others and enables discovering their beliefs and experiences. There is no final answer as a result. As we go down this journey of discovery, the definition of what is right keeps evolving with new contexts.

"Preach what you practice," should be the mantra—not, "Practice what you preach." The mantra's essence lies in paying attention to seeing self, seeing others, and seeing context. Wherever we show up, our whole self comes along.

My parents wanted a son. I, finally, got myself.

We are always more than we present, more than we know, and more than we can control.

Shelly Dhamija

SHELLY DHAMIJA is a friend, mentor, and a life coach. As an Organizational Development professional and engineering-focused leader, she brings a unique mix of people- and engineering-mindsets to empowering and enabling teams to deliver optimum solutions and to become better versions of themselves. She leads with compassion, embraces life with positivity and grace, and gives back to her community and those around her with a resilient spirit and a warm heart.

NINE

Itchy Bumps

Chris L. Johnson, PsyD

On a hot and humid August in Chicago I developed a set of painful and embarrassing symptoms: red itchy bumps all over my upper thighs that were constantly itching to the point of keeping me up at night scratching.

I had been invited to teach a series of stress management courses at a large bank in Chicago. And yet here I was, uncomfortable and out of sorts. The symptoms had gone on for a few weeks, despite the application of topical creams, and I couldn't stand it any longer. I begrudgingly consulted my doctor. I'd convinced myself that I'd developed an allergy because I could think of nothing—nothing physical, at least—that was different in those few weeks: no new detergent, no poison ivy from hiking, no nothing.

I had developed skills working with addiction, stress, and traumatic stress—and while working at the Employee Resource Center early in my career I had blended these with my keen interest in supporting healthy and thriving workplaces. The prevailing view of stress then was that it was unavoidable and ultimately bad. Intuitively of course, this made sense. When we're stressed we tell ourselves to get a hold of, loosen the grip on, or manage our stress reactions. Yet in those moments we're at the biological mercy of the threat trifecta—fight, flight, or freeze. Conventional wisdom on working with stress centered around traditional cognitive interventions: identifying stresses, learning to counter stress beliefs with mental challenges, then creating a plan to mitigate stressful outcomes. As if it were that easy.

This is what I was preparing to help people at the bank address.

After conducting a series of allergy tests the doctor concluded that I was suffering from a severe case of contact dermatitis, an unpleasant and painful situation that typically remits after two to four weeks of treatment. This explained my symptoms.

The doctor's diagnosis? Chronic stress. To add insult to personal injury, the good doctor dared to recommend a stress management program for me. The gall.

I was not happy.

I was convinced she was wrong. *I am decidedly not stressed*, I thought to myself. I harrumphed my way out of her office with a Benadryl script in hand. But I didn't address my underlying stress.

The itchy bumps took just shy of a month to clear up and all the while I was befuddled at my doctor's recommendation. Was her diagnosis accurate? Could I be more stressed than I realized? Surely not.

Only in hindsight could I see that working two jobs, completing an advanced degree, dealing with the emotional aftermath of my sister's recent brutal assault, and purchasing my first home, ranked me high on Rahe's Stress Scale.

But my body knew, if only I had listened. *I didn't know how.* I couldn't see my experience because:

- The story I was telling myself was that I could and should handle it all. The diagnosis revealed what I considered a personal weakness.
- I believed that my hard work and extra hours would prevail in my drive to meet my goals. I was attached to my belief about working hard, though I couldn't see it

then, and this contributed to my body's manifestation of stress symptoms.

- My beliefs overrode my own emotional responses to these accumulating stressors. While I'd have denied it then, my emotional awareness and range were constrictcd; I was all up in my head simply attempting to cope.
- I hadn't taken the time to reflect and to listen to what my body knew to be true—that I was experiencing overload and my body needed more attention from me. Contact dermatitis sure got my attention!

In my continued preparation to teach the stress management class, while trying not to scratch my legs raw, I came across the book *Full Catastrophe Living.*[1] I learned of a new approach to stress—simply pausing to be with the symptoms of stress versus attempting to manage them. I remember thinking, *What a novel idea—maybe I can learn from this too.* I started experimenting with this mindful approach and I found that by being with what showed up for me—initially my feelings toward the itchy bumps—they would start to subside. I began to relax, and became less worried about performance or making a difference. This approach so resonated with me that I incorporated the book's teachings into my class material.

Learning to be with and accept my own experiences fully—itchy bumps, tender and tragic emotions, ingrained beliefs, life's uncertainties—without trying to control, manage, or change them proved to be a threshold experience for me. In fact it set the professional trajectory of my career.

Not only was a mindful approach more effective in dealing with stress, it unlocked the door to greater awareness, self-compassion, and presence. Initially I felt off and out of my element. Curious but raw, my feelings were at a remove, my beliefs powerful obstacles to connecting deeply to my heart. Vulnerability had been tucked away beneath a guise of composure and competence. As a teacher once shared with me, feeling undone is our unfolding. My healing unfolded in fits and starts. These tender moments, held within a supportive practice community, blossomed. In subsequent years, as a mindfulness practitioner and educator, I've been able to support others in their stresses and suffering, particularly at work.

Three key lessons from my journey stand out:

- Where we put our attention matters. Mind the gap.
- We grow our capacity and presence by accepting the realities at hand. Face, feel, free—repeat.
- Listening to the wisdom of our bodies is *the* key to cultivating compassion in working with ourselves and others.

Only recently has the science offered new insights into what happens when we meet up with pressure, stress and suffering. Dr Kelly McGonigal, a professor of health sciences at Stanford, once a true believer in the saga that "stress is bad"[2], developed a popular course called *The New Science of Stress*. There we learned that we're physiologically wired for more than just the three threat stress reactions of fight, flight, and freeze. We humans have successfully adapted our stress responses over time to function more effectively in modern life. Believing that stress is an enhancing challenge response, we can access our energy to *respond* instead of *reacting* out of fear.

We're fueled by a complex cascade of stress hormones that regulate our biology, reduce self-focus, and dial up awareness of the precursors to compassion: the distress and pain of those around us. High oxytocin bolsters our courage and motivates us to protect the people and communities we care about. Focused but not fearful, we tend to bounce back faster too, with less lingering distress. Our strong emotions serve the neurobiological conditions for new learning; resilience grows. That may be why leaders with a strong presence can read a room, feel into an audience, pick up cues of emotional valence in others, and move into right action—especially in response to suffering. A challenge response is compassion-in-action. Exactly what I was hoping to teach to the stress management class.

PAUL WAS REFERRED to me as a possible candidate for the mindfulness class I'd soon be teaching. A hulk of a man—tall and wide with a booming voice—he owned a small business that he had built up through sheer will and grit. Pride and weariness edged his voice as he told me how he'd systematically built his business over twenty years, employing more than a hundred people. By typical standards, Paul was a successful guy.

Yet in my office his bulky frame slumped on my couch, his affect flat, his despair palpable. His life was coming undone. I could feel the depth of his pain though I didn't yet know the extent of his suffering. His biggest complaint—besides his staff not respecting him and his wife browbeating him about long office hours—was that he'd not slept a good night's sleep for years, literally.

Paul was desperate for relief. His therapist thought that the mindfulness class I was teaching to develop resilience skills might help him address his long-term PTSD symptoms too: anger, trouble concentrating, hypervigilance, disrupted sleep. Towards his goal of sleeping through the night he was willing to try just about anything.

The first class involves a getting-to-know-you component comprised of a breath practice and open circle discussion. When Paul spoke, bitterness and blame about his life, his business, and his inability to sleep spewed into the space. Some classmates shirked back in sharp reaction to his energy.

Over the next month, Paul required me to be fully present as he explored the depth of his pain, and to create the space to hold what he himself was struggling to contain while also challenging him to learn to *be with it* too. He practiced during the week yet he baited me with questions, projecting his experiences outward in blame and inward to self-loathing. He didn't want to feel, despite growing awareness that he was, indeed, already feeling.

Paul struggled, as we all do, to feel himself, his body, his sensations, and the fullness of his emotions. Feeling deeply is fundamental to being human, a part of our natural intelligence. Yet emotions are typically resistant to being addressed simply on a rational level, like in traditional stress classes. Instead, deep in the cerebral cortex the insula registers incoming sensory data from our bodies. By feeling into these bodily sensations we open up greater access to difficult emotional information and expand our emotional range and capacity. This neural guidance system helps us listen deeply, gauge trust, and create resonance with others—not something accessible with a cognitive shift alone.

In quiet moments of noticing breath and body in our class time, Paul was learning to pause and be present with the panoply of his experiences and the anxiety, guilt, and anger that accompanied them. By facing himself fully, he was freeing himself of the need to fight or avoid or push away the reality at hand. He was more responsive and less reactively bound to his old coping strategies. Befriending his experiences as allies instead of enemies contributed to his healing. And slowly, despite himself, his nervous system began to settle, his guard relaxed, his attention to others became more open. Paul was minding the gap.

Of course, each of us is familiar with the all-too-human tendency *to not* be present to our moments at hand. My stint at the bank all those years ago had shown me how susceptible I was to not noticing my body, feelings, and impact on others. Often our emotional experiences are sticky and distressing. Mine certainly were!

We learned in bits and pieces that Paul's business, and his leadership, were largely shaped by his time leading troops in Vietnam as a young man. His gruff, barking manner had worked there—it moved his men into action. Dodging active combat fire generated a deep bond of care between them. Back home in the United States, however, barking orders at his current employees— well that didn't work so well. It didn't show his employees "care" at all. Quite the opposite: they were afraid of him.

The emotional underpinnings of life and death that he'd experienced in Vietnam were driving his current sense-making and decisions about working with people. If you'd asked him he'd have told you that he cared deeply about his employees, that they were "like family to me." Yet his abrupt and reactive behaviors had taken center stage, obscuring his tender heart from them. He'd tearfully confessed a few weeks into the course: "I'm afraid I'm letting everyone down, could that be why I can't sleep?"

His question hung suspended while Paul felt its weight. The silence of collective presence was deafening. His classmates were listening, feeling, and holding space for him. He was learning to face, feel, and then free the emotions he tried so hard to contain.

SUCH EMBODIED LEARNING is less about acquiring knowledge— where the focus is on teachers talking and students listening—and more about being able to feel one's self in the moment. It begins by situating the body as the essential place of learning, action, and— ultimately—of transformation. Such presence is enlivening, contagious even. The energy generated opens wounds, tight places, and closed hearts, as people practice together in all their humanity.

In class, in this shared context, people feel seen by the instructor and by each other, all attuned to nuances of body, breath, story. People *feel felt*, as though there's a spotlight shining on them that somehow extends to includes others.

Because it does.

This quality of presence involves the capacity to hold attention on one's self, concerns, and sensations while simultaneously paying full attention to another(s), in the same moment, without distraction. The distinction of simultaneous attention is important because the neural networks for embodied self-awareness are the same as the neural networks for empathy and compassion.

Over the course of a few short weeks Paul's heart began to soften, visibly. One evening during our check-in Paul choked up and, teary-eyed, exclaimed: "I've been able to sleep through the night this week!" His classmates cheered! In the final week of class, during a body scan practice, Paul began to doze, a gentle snore at the back of the room.

Compassion isn't an idea; it manifests in our bodies and shifts our chemistry by reducing cortisol and increasing oxytocin, both key stress hormones. Compassionate presence emerges. We become more open, curious, and responsive—eager to join in conversations that matter and to take actions that support others. This quality of presence is a manifestation of compassion-in-action.

Chris L. Johnson, PsyD

Chris L. Johnson is founder of Q4Consulting, dedicated to cultivating strong leaders, healthy workplaces, and thriving communities. As a psychologist, executive coach, and mindfulness educator, she integrates evidence-based neuroscience with body-based wisdom to create powerful and transformative learning environments. Her first book, The Leadership Pause, focuses on business health and wellbeing for conscious leaders. She lives in Chicago with her husband where they are active in the Chicago chapter of Conscious Capitalism.

TEN

It's Just Business

Quentin Finney

"Nothing personal, it's just business" he said two decades ago, laying me off with only two weeks of severance pay and benefits less than a month before the birth of my daughter.

Nothing personal.

On top of feeling the pure shock of the news, those five words cut right into the heart of the matter, right into *my* heart, and while unfortunately that wasn't the last time I would hear those five words in the world of work, I could go the rest of my life without ever having to hear them again.

As I sat there listening to him pontificate about how one of his own layoff experiences led him to the best role he'd ever had, how things like this were actually good for a person's career, my mouth watered. I worked to hold my center while my whole body vacillated between strong impulses for fight and flight responses. I'm sure my jaw was tight and hard as a brick.

Was this real? Though I had contributed my fair share of blood, sweat and tears in my role, was I actually viewed as disposable?

When someone says, "nothing personal, it's just business," in the middle of a life-changing conversation like a layoff, the words land like the cold, wet Chicago wind of my youth, cutting straight through everything on the surface and hitting deeply, right down into muscle and bone in a way that makes your whole body shudder. I felt as though all the years of effort, commitment, and contributions were being dismissed, reduced to a transactional decision that clearly didn't consider the possible impact on me, the affected human on the receiving end—right down to the way the news was delivered. As is common for many of us, facing a complete lack of meaningful information I started to tell myself stories about what was happening—stories that didn't just try to explain the situation but that amplified the intense pain and fear that I was feeling in that moment.

My first born was due in a month, and I was only left with two weeks of benefits.

Perhaps I wasn't good enough. Perhaps I didn't really matter, I thought. My heart and mind spiraled in a hurricane of thought and emotion, replaying moments where I wondered if I could have done more or been even more visible, and feeling growing anger that I couldn't see any balance between the positive revenue impacts I knew clearly I'd created and the 'reward' of being laid off apparently for convenience, with no reason given. I started to believe that the years I spent pouring my energy into the mission weren't truly seen or valued—that I was just a cog in the grinding machine, a disembodied 'human resource', easily replaced.

I also wondered about the deeper dynamics that might be at play in the lack of shared rationale: *clearly, decisions were being made behind closed doors that I'll never understand, as my performance reviews were all solid. Did I misstep in ways I wasn't even aware of, ways that were never shared with me?* The lack of explanation or acknowledgment further fueled strong feelings of betrayal.

Worst of all, I started internalizing these thoughts, for a period of time feeling them erode my confidence and sense of self-worth. In moments like these, we can easily feel invisible, stripped of the self-identity we've built through our work. That phrase "nothing personal, it's just business," was clearly intended to create insulating distance for the speaker, yet for the receiving listener those words plant the seeds of self-doubt and shame in fertile ground—a stark reminder of how words, even casual ones, can shape the stories we create about ourselves and our value.

The dehumanizing impact of "it's just business"

I think we as leaders should make a real effort to purge that five-word saying from our lexicon altogether.

Nothing personal, it's just business.

Who are those words meant for and what are they meant to convey? Who are they meant to comfort? How are we so blind to the reality that the impact on the person hearing those words is always personal, regardless of context leading the speaker to say them?

In my view, statements like this only serve as a convenient shield for the person saying them, a way to absolve themselves of guilt or discomfort in delivering difficult news. Such an approach distances them from the very real and personal impact on the person they're addressing, as if saying "it's just business" somehow lessens the blow, somehow makes the personal impact less visible (or even, altogether invisible).

Really understanding the gravity of this phrase requires breaking down the consequences of holding this kind of detached mindset. When a leader says "nothing personal," they're actually signaling a broader issue: a refusal to recognize or acknowledge that there is a human being who will be affected by the difficult business decision being made and executed.

Consider common situations in which this phrase is most often invoked: layoffs, restructuring, unfavorable shifts, and other painful pivots. For those on the receiving end of these five words, such events are not just business; they ripple straight into their personal lives, affecting everything from financial stability to personal mental health—for themselves, and for their families and loved ones. The repercussions of these actions go far beyond a job title or paycheck, yet there's a pervasive belief in many industry verticals that emotional detachment is synonymous with professionalism. But this mindset not only damages individual lives; it can harm entire organizations for large periods of time in the court of public opinion.

When employees feel like they're disposable, that sense erodes trust, loyalty, engagement and overall morale—things every company needs to succeed and thrive.

Why compassion belongs in business

I'm not at all suggesting that making difficult decisions is something that should be avoided. I'm suggesting that as leaders we're required to walk the fine line of balance between making the critical hard decisions that absolutely need to be made—while equally honoring and respecting the dignity of the people who will be affected by those decisions and how they're carried out. A more empathetic, compassionate leadership approach would recognize that each decision, no matter how small, affects real people with complex lives outside today's world of work. When difficult news needs to be delivered, such leaders don't hide behind dismissive phrases. Instead, they take responsibility for their choices, acknowledging the hardships created, and being as transparent as possible about the circumstances demanding the decision being made.

Compassionate leaders create environments where people feel valued for more than just their output, where they feel valued for who they are and for how they're moving through the world by the contributions they make. These leaders prioritize open communication and are willing to engage in difficult conversations, not as a formality, but as an opportunity to support and understand their team members.

When employees feel respected and understood, they're more resilient in times of change, and change is the great constant. Companies with high-trust cultures, where empathy and compassion are practiced at all levels, consistently enjoy higher engagement, greater productivity, and lower turnover. The caring human touch isn't just a nice addition to business—it's a critical ingredient for our long-term success.

Practical steps for empathetic decision-making

So how can we, as leaders, start to move beyond "nothing personal" and embrace a more compassionate approach?

1. **Acknowledge the personal impact.** When delivering difficult news, start by recognizing the personal impact. Flip the script and imagine how the news would feel if you were the one receiving it, which unlocks the ability for a more empathetic framing for how you'll deliver the news. Skillfully engaging in an honest, direct and respectful way allows the affected human a better chance to feel into their own dignity and move forward. Remember that "just business" almost always creates a devastating impact, and it doesn't have to be that way.

2. **Share the reason and rationale.** Being as transparent as possible about why a decision was made can help reduce feelings of confusion and betrayal. Avoid sugarcoating or ambiguous statements, as they can come across as insincere in a moment where relational connection is necessary. When people better understand the "why" behind a decision, they're more likely to respect the process, even if they're unhappy with the outcome.

3. **Invite feedback, even if it's critical.** Allow everyone to express their concerns and feelings without fear of retribution. Open dialogue also can be a powerful tool for maintaining trust among those who weren't impacted and remain in their seats. A necessary decision executed poorly might harm company culture in the long term if people widely feel undervalued or disposable—and the corollary impact on retention and engagement can't be understated.

Balancing hard business decisions with human dignity

Sometimes, hard business decisions must be made, no doubt. Budgets need to be managed, missions change in response to market demands, teams need to be restructured, even entire departments are reorganized in response. Often, changes are necessary for the very survival of the business, and the blow-back for not making them can be even more painful.

Compassionate leadership is not about making the decisions easier: it's about making the decisions kinder.

If anything, the more difficult the decision, the more necessary it becomes to handle it with kindness and care. The way we deliver hard news matters just as much as the decision itself. Choosing to approach these conversations with respect, acknowledging the personal impact of the news being delivered, and supporting the person through the transition are a good start. Other seemingly small acts of respect—a sincere apology, a moment of empathy, a willingness to listen—can go a long way in helping people feel valued, even in the midst of what may be an incredibly difficult time for them.

What if we were to show that we see the individual, not just the job? Is anything truly lost by making that choice? What could the world of work be like if we dipped into self-awareness and examined our own biases and beliefs with an eye on modulating how we execute necessary things in the kindest and most compassionate way possible – all the time?

If we truly want to lead differently, with integrity and humanity, we must answer the long asked call to move beyond the "nothing personal" mentality. The business world doesn't have to be an emotionless battlefield where people are pitted against profit. Instead, it can be a space where empathy and compassion coexist with efficiency, where leaders understand that every decision affects people's lives in very real ways – and they find the balance point.

Imagine a world where no one ever again felt the need to say, "nothing personal, it's just business." Imagine a workplace where decisions are made with both the head and the heart. For some, this emerging vision may seem idealistic, but I believe it's achievable—and necessary—for the benefit of all. Tomorrow's leaders have a real chance to take a stand and redefine what right action means in a professional context, moving from a cold, impersonal approach to one fully rooted in humanity and compassion—one that cares about those being led with as much care as accomplishing the mission.

May it be so.

Quentin Finney

QUENTIN FINNEY is a human, father, best-selling author, international certified mindfulness teacher, member of the Forbes Coaches Council, and long-time meditation practitioner. After holding operational and executive leadership roles with organizations including Google, Red Hat, EMC, and six startups, he has spent the last decade consulting and coaching, helping others as they discover the inner wisdom they don't always recognize they have—and he firmly believes we're just not meant to do any of this alone.

ELEVEN

Taking Flight

Orlando White

My story begins where many like mine often do—in the uncertain moments before life's cocoon separates us from the sun.

In the early months of 2023 I found myself in a conference room that I had walked by countless times. Often occupied by larger teams for offsites or workshops, it never struck me as anything more than just another room in the company where I'd spent the last eight years. That day it became the setting for my undoing.

Sitting in the boardroom-style meeting room, I looked across the table at my manager, who was there in person. The Vice President of my organization joined virtually, followed by a member of Human Resources.

"Orlando, we've appreciated your contributions," my Vice President began, "but we feel your role would be a better fit on another team at LinkedIn. There's an opportunity there for you, and we hope you choose to take it. But if you decide to leave, we'll provide support to ensure a smooth transition to your next play."

My heart raced with uncertainty.

"Orlando, this is your choice," my Vice President continued. "But we need an answer by Monday."

The gravity connecting my feet to the earth released; time seemed to turn inside out or to fold in on itself. My world as I had come to know it began to unravel. LinkedIn wasn't just where I started my career—it was a refuge. It gave me the resources to create a life and claim a freedom my younger self could have only dreamed of. All of that was now at stake. My fear made it hard to breathe, as if my lungs had to search for the next breath before it arrived.

Within the depths of my trepidation I could hear a gentle voice whispering to me, *It's time.* The voice confirmed what my heart already knew: it was time to leave. The days and weeks that followed were a whirlwind of farewell emails, lunches, and LinkedIn posts.

Then came the silence.

The first Monday without my job hit me profoundly.

What am I supposed to do now? I asked myself. In the suspended quiet, the person I had known myself to be fell apart. Waves of anticipation, fear, and self-criticism washed over me like rivers. There were moments that felt unbearable, yet every so often that same quiet inner voice would resurface and ground me. It would appear in the kind words of a stranger, in a loving reminder from a mentor, in the stoic stillness of the redwoods. Something was waiting for me on the other side of this unraveling, though I couldn't see it yet. In the darkness of the unknown I reached out to my community for guidance. One of them, a trusted advisor, spoke to me about a coach he knew: Raven.

"She's brilliant," he told me. "She'll push you in ways that will make you grow. She'll support you in ways that no one else will."

His words were filled with admiration and I trusted his judgment. He initiated the introduction. Within hours Raven emailed me directly to set up our first meeting. There was something about the speed of her response, the confidence in the work she's done to help others, that left an impression. But beneath my optimism there was a subtle and uneasy feeling that I couldn't shake. My gut sensed something—a slight tension I couldn't name but which lingered in the background, quiet and insistent. I brushed it aside, eager to receive any help I could get, and convinced myself that this was a necessary step in my growth. After all, I had been told Raven was the best. And yet the feeling remained.

When she joined the Zoom meeting she greeted me with an energized, "Hello." Her voice was punctuated by a noticeable Canadian accent and her energy felt familiar, as though we'd met before. She began by asking me about myself and my interests. I shared my passion for helping others and spoke about my career in community engagement. I told her about my meditation practice, how I first discovered the power of the breath while a student at Howard University— how my practice deepened over the years and eventually led me to earn a teaching certification to guide others. Raven listened intently, nodding.

"You have so much light in you," she said, her words feeling both affirming and sincere. She shared that she'd started guiding others at my age as well, which filled me with hope that she could support me in the next stage of my journey. I also spoke about my tendency to doubt myself, explaining that I would need a coach who could motivate me when I felt uncertain or wanted to play small. She reassured me that she would be my champion, that my success was now a part of her mission.

Even with her confidence in supporting me, I had difficulty ignoring a lingering hesitancy. Something in me urged caution but I wondered if this might be an opportunity to heal—a chance to release some of the lingering pain I still carried from grade school. Those years often felt like navigating through a minefield, searching for any glimmer of my own brilliance in what I was learning and who I was learning it from.

I decided to trust her to guide me.

We began meeting biweekly, each session starting in a similar way. She'd ask how I was doing and I'd share what I was feeling. She became a trusted confidante, supporting me through the challenging moments that I could no longer escape by immersing myself in work. Our sessions were almost exclusively online. The first time I met her in person was at her home in the Berkeley Hills. She had a large house with white walls, a wooden piano, and a big south-facing bay window that in the light of sunset seemed to illuminate. I was feeling particularly low this day, still contending with what my next steps would be. She had me stand in the center of her living room while she held a drum in her left hand and a drumstick in her right. She began beating the drum, its powerful vibration filling each corner of her home.

"My name is Raven," she started, "and I carry the light."

She said it with a certainty that awakened something within me. She walked around her living room beating the drum. She walked closer to where I was standing, looked me right in the eyes, and repeated her words louder this time.

"My name is Raven. I carry the light." She then looked at me, handed me the drum and said, "Your turn."

I took the drum in my hand, feeling a bit awkward about having to chant my own name, but I decided to stay open and curious. I began to beat the drum, gradually finding a rhythm that felt natural.

"My name is Orlando White," I started. "And I carry the light."

She looked at me and said, "Again."

"My name is Orlando White," I repeated. "And I carry the light."

"Once more," she urged, holding my gaze.

"My name is Orlando White," I shouted, feeling defiance rise within me. "And I carry the light."

I felt fire flowing through me.

"This is your power," she said.

I reply, "I feel it. I've experienced it at various points in my life. But I often find it easier to play small than to fully embrace it. And I don't want to make anyone uncomfortable."

"Well people will just have to get used to it," she responded firmly.

I looked at her and felt permission to no longer cower or shrink myself to make others comfortable. She reminded me that the fire I was feeling had always been there.

In the months that followed we continued our biweekly cadence of virtual meetings. I'd share what was happening in my life and the steps I was taking to grow as a teacher; she'd share personal anecdotes or provide recommendations to support me. After our first series of work together ended, she asked if I wanted to continue working with her.

"You've made such incredible progress, and I am so excited for what's next. If you choose to continue working with me, your trajectory as a teacher will only accelerate from here. I've seen this so many times," she promised.

I reflected on the support that she had offered me in the three months we'd worked together and decided to continue with the program.

As winter melted into spring I continued teaching on my own while also attending retreats and networking with other mindfulness leaders. Though our virtual calls persisted, I had high hopes that this next phase of our collaboration would provide me with direct guidance from her on how to lead others effectively. Unfortunately that support wasn't happening.

On a gentle summer day, she sent me a text asking if I'd be interested in assisting her with a meditation retreat she would be leading. A jolt of excitement coursed through me, as this was the level of support I had been hoping for. I replied enthusiastically, telling her that I'd love to support her and to please share what she needed. She responded that we'd hop on a call to discuss logistics. The next day I eagerly joined the Zoom call, thrilled at the chance to organize a retreat together and learn from her.

When she joined she greeted me as usual then said, "So, I'm thinking of doing a retreat in July. Do you think we'd be able to pull something together by then?"

I glanced at the calendar, noting that it was already mid-June, but felt confident in her experience as a teacher. Surely we could organize something quickly.

"Do you have anyone we could invite?" she asked.

Confusion hit me. I had assumed she had a number of clients of her own—she often made a point of mentioning it.

"Do you not have folks we could invite?" I replied, puzzled.

"No," she said sternly. "I don't have connections deep enough in the Bay Area to invite people to a retreat. That's why I reached out to you for assistance. I thought you'd help me recruit attendees."

"Well, I would be happy to help, but if I extended the invite to my community, I would like to hold that space with you." I looked at her with calm bewilderment and considered how the folks in my life would expect me to lead if I invited them to a retreat.

I could feel her anger growing as she yelled: "No! I would never teach with you. You aren't ready to be a teacher! I do not teach with my students!" I felt my heart race as I processed her words, the weight of her dismissal hanging heavily in the air.

"Raven," I said, struggling to understand what was happening, "this isn't just about me. It's about creating a space that honors the participants who'll be involved. If we're going to do this with my community, I need to be an equal part of it."

"You're wasting my time," she yelled. "I need to leave. You think you're ready, but you're not ready."

She abruptly exited the Zoom call, leaving me in stunned silence. It was the last time I would ever speak to her.

My heart raced as I processed her words, each one cutting deeper than I expected. I sat in front of my screen and stared at my reflection. I closed my eyes and took a breath—feelings of anger, confusion, and loss illuminated a pathway in my heart. I took a step and find a small boy curled in a corner. Tears are streaming down his face.

"What if she's right?" he asks me. "What if she's just like my teachers?"

I take the boy's hands in mine and look in his eyes. I can see myself reflected in him. "Those teachers are wrong," I tell him. "And so is Raven."

Raven's denial lit the way to the child in me—the child who learned that taking up space was dangerous, who felt like he needed to cower to make others comfortable. She lit the path so I could find him and hold him in my arms tightly. It was the embracing of him that shattered her, and every rejection of me. My anger lifted and I found a new way home. That light supported me in hosting my first retreat in celebration of Oakland Pride. It also led me to hold a sacred water ceremony with my community to celebrate my thirty-first birthday.

What if rejection from others is instead an invitation to reach within? In asking that question, little me begins to glow in golden light.

This time he takes my hand and says with a smile, *"It's time to fly —again."*

Orlando White

ORLANDO WHITE believes that mindfulness and radical authenticity are essential pathways to our collective wholeness. He is the founder of Overflow, a program dedicated to helping individuals reclaim their true selves, those from before they learned to hide behind a mask. His mission focuses on the holistic well-being of those of us who are often left at the margins. An award-winning community engagement strategist and certified mindfulness teacher, Orlando is also a proud graduate of Howard University.

The Power in Empathy

If you believe in compassion, in non-harming, in kindness, in wisdom, in generosity, in calmness, in solitude, in non-doing, in being even-handed and clear, do you manifest these qualities in your daily life?[1]

Jon Kabat-Zinn

TWELVE

From Heroes to WeRose

Jochen Raysz

G lancing around the staff room in the retreat center, I saw that my biggest fear had materialized. Tears were rolling down Mary's cheeks. Tim was staring into space. Tamara was fidgeting with her fingers and desperately trying to avoid looking at anyone else. Everyone reacted to the news we had just shared in their own way, but the shock, sadness, and fear were written in everyone's face. The future of what had felt like our new home was suddenly completely uncertain.

A few days earlier, Magnus, the operator of our Sweden-based retreat center, had asked to meet with me and my partner, Kathy. The three of us had been running the retreat center since taking it over eleven months ago. It had quickly become a symbol for the flourishing of our global community and organization. We had waiting lists for retreats and many were eager to volunteer for renovation projects, landscaping, or tending to the small organic farm.

It felt like a dream come true to have a place where everyone's practice could be integrated and demonstrated in real-world daily life through their unique passions and gifts. That dream now seemed to have come to an abrupt end.

Kathy and I both could feel Magnus' utter discomfort as he was grappling to find the right words to tell us that he was going to move on. He had met someone and wanted to refocus his energy and resources to a new project. I was shocked. We had worked so hard together to create all of this, put so much care, time, money, and sweat into it. How could he leave? To make things worse he was looking to transition all his responsibilities within the next month. Magnus had been the superhero who had funded the place initially and every month magically made the finances work out. He had a gift for identifying key areas to renovate and the experience to get it done masterfully. How could we possibly buy him out and run this place without him? How would the people react? Would they lose confidence and leave as well?

I spent the rest of the day in a daze with a million thoughts racing through my head. The sinking feeling in my gut only got worse with every attempt to understand what had happened and what to do next. I took a long, aimless walk through the forest. My entire being mirrored the bleak and damp November grey of the Swedish countryside.

THINGS OFTEN LOOK and feel better for me after a good night's sleep. The next morning I began moving into action. I had been Head of Global Operations for our organization for a couple of years. During these early years as a startup this fancy title often meant that I was literally 'doing the stuff.' Over a few cups of espresso, I began making lists of questions that we needed to answer, decisions we needed to make, challenges and ways to solve them. Focusing on what I could do and how I could serve helped me to not drown in sadness and lose myself in worst-case scenarios.

As we often do, Kathy and I took a strategy walk to go over everything we'd have to do in the coming days. The scariest question on my mind was how were we going to share the news with everyone without stirring up pain over the loss of a trusted leader and friend, and without instilling fear of an uncertain future? Who would put their hearts and minds at ease? Usually that's the job of the hero. But the hero was leaving.

Gradually, as we played out different scenarios, a vision emerged of how the momentum of this shakeup could be harnessed to create a new version of our center—a center that would be more resilient and in even greater alignment with our vision of inspiring and empowering people to tap into their full potential. What if everyone could become the hero of this new era?

The meeting in the staff room was the initiation into our collective hero's journey. From our experience of overcoming personal challenges, Kathy and I knew that accessing our full potential as a team would require us to get real with the circumstance, with ourselves, with each other. We started by sharing the facts, the implications, and what was at stake.

We did not pretend that we had all the answers or that we were certain of a positive outcome. Instead of trying to protect our team from the painful emotions and dreadful thoughts, we invited everyone to hold space for each other and to allow those who wanted to share what was on their minds and hearts to do so. We joined in and were open about what it was really like for us. We knew this would give others permission to do the same. Instead of letting the dark stuff linger in the background, we brought it to the light. Having a permission field to name what was really happening was extremely freeing and empowering—it liberated the transformational power in emotions we usually try to avoid.

Our situation hadn't changed, but the atmosphere shifted from gloomy inertia to a sense of deep connection and gradually it gave rise to passionate dedication. Everyone shared how much the past eleven months had meant to them and nobody was going to give up. The space opened to talk about action plans, new roles and responsibilities, and what each of us would focus on to make it happen.

The following weeks were intense. This was November 2008, the height of the financial crisis. Not an ideal time to go out and find money for a retreat center in the Swedish countryside. One bank did not even reply to our inquiry. Mary volunteered to spearhead our search for funding and to get started with cashflow analysis and forecasting.

Much of the knowledge required for the center's daily operations—the critical infrastructure of its four large buildings, its heating systems, its water management—were in Magnus' mind only. There had never been a need to systematize this information so we had to start from scratch. This was going to be Tamara's focus.

Other already existing roles expanded from merely executing Magnus' directives to having full responsibility for their respective area.

For most on the team, taking on this kind of ownership was a new experience with its own set of challenges. Having responsibility and the authority to make decisions can be experienced as empowering but also as a burden. In addition to all the stuff that had to get done, there was also the looming uncertainty of the outcome of all our efforts—while coming to terms with the fact that a close friend and ally had left us.

I remember starting many conversations by asking, "How are you? I mean, how are you *really*?" Kathy and I gave each other the same space to initiate a moment of pause and self-reflection. Where are your energy levels? What's weighing on you, and what's inspiring you?

I began listening as much to my heart and gut as I did to my mind. I connected more with the different energies around and within me and grew to trust my inner voice. I would send a text or call a person who frequently came to mind, because I knew there must be a reason for why I was thinking about them. Having a shared vision, mission, and values is a great start—but it's these kind of daily actions and conversations that really bring them alive.

We grew closer and stronger as a team, which gave everyone even more freedom to explore their unique ways of doing what they do best. The more transparent that people were with how they were *actually* doing, rather than just ploughing through their task lists, the more natural it became to offer and ask for help. We all felt that we were in this together.

As a highly empathic person, these were among the toughest moments in my professional life. I had learned different ways of drawing boundaries by withdrawing or by blocking the feelings in a room when they got too intense. To be most skillful, this circumstance asked me to be completely willing to feel everything fully, to let the energy move through me, to digest it and metabolize it so that my response could come from a place of authentic connection and real understanding.

People knew what we all were processing. Spoken or unspoken, the atmosphere was communicating, "I feel it too," or, "I am here with you."

Showing up with strength and confidence had been one of the unquestioned must-haves in my self-image as a leader. During these days, I noticed how these qualities had also served as a protective shield to hide my fears and insecurities. How could I expect the people on our team to open up if I didn't show up with an equal amount of vulnerability? How could they trust it was safe to express what was really going on with them if they never heard about my own challenges?

Back in 2008, I did not have any role-models for the power of vulnerability in my life or career. From an early age I had learned to divide people into weak or strong, and strong people didn't talk about their challenges (or feelings for that matter) in real-time. Now I had to find a deeper strength, the courage to lower my guard and show more of my human side.

It was an opportunity to integrate my practice into more and more moments of life. Remembering and resting in the indestructible essence of my being was my go-to foundation for holding space for everyone, including myself. Recognizing that this essence was strong and steady regardless of the wild thoughts and emotions that were coming up in me, I could see it and reflect it back to those around me.

The more I trusted and relied on this solid core, the more vulnerability I could allow for myself and others. With every conversation in which I was willing to reveal more of myself, I received more trust as a leader, not less. The same has proven true as a friend, a son, a husband, or a coach. Strength and vulnerability are a powerful pair.

Our principles of transparency and participation, and our practice of asking for help rippled into the wider community of people who had been to the retreat center. They knew what we were up to, and there was always someone willing to step up or who could introduce us to people and resources we needed.

That's how we heard about a small bank specializing in supporting causes like ours. Working with them required us to incorporate as a non-profit which we all felt was a perfect fit. Another requirement was to find micro-guarantors for the mortgage. Each of them would need to vouch for the center with a small amount of their personal funds. We had no problem reaching the target to get the mortgage.

The ease of this process demonstrated how getting everyone on board initially, and seeing each other in our humanity, had created a ripple effect of trust, dedication, and commitment. The shared sense of ownership grew far beyond the walls of the center. This bond carried us through many challenges in the following years. When travel restrictions and lockdowns during the pandemic led to a near-complete loss of income for two years, updates to the community about the center's needs opened a stream of donations that made it possible to continue operating.

Magnus was not the last person to decide to move on. But we have come to see that the culture and organizational systems can accommodate difficult changes and transitions, and that while everyone is an integral part of the whole, no one is completely indispensable. As a leader myself, I find that very liberating.

Almost twenty years later, the story that is alive and shared at the campfire is not about one hero who turned things around. It's about how all of us together have risen to the occasion. We don't know what will happen with the center in a world where so many activities are shifting to online learning and virtual communities. But our center has grown to be far more than the physical space. It's a symbol of the power of connection, trust, and perseverance. It's the proof that if we stick together there is nothing we cannot do.

Jochen Raysz

JOCHEN RAYSZ supports leaders and coaches in developing inner sustainability and living fully aligned with their deepest essence, values, and purpose as they drive meaningful change in their organizations and the world. His coaching integrates meditation practices that seamlessly blend into daily life and workplaces, alongside tools from psychology, neuroscience, and his experience as a co-founder and executive in impact-driven organizations in Europe and the US.

THIRTEEN

Lights! Camera! Engagement!

Erem Latif

I n many of my professional roles over the years I've struggled with reporting to leaders or managers I didn't click with or with whom it was difficult to establish a rapport. At times I would fixate on this dynamic, wondering if it was me, or them—trying to determine how I could rectify the relationship. This was natural for the young professional I was at the time.

Most of us have learned, either through personal experience or therapy, or—let's admit it— the last TV series or movie we watched, that relationships are based on give and take, the proverbial two-way street. So each of us must take partial ownership for every relationship we participate in, personal or professional.

Ultimately, we get to decide how we are showing up in these relationships. We can be conscious, heart-centered, and aligned with good intentions and compassion. Or we can show up reactionary, derisive, and emotion-forward.

But what must also be recognized is that our jobs, our professional lives, and the business world as a whole create a separate ecosystem of professional relationships that may not have been as deeply examined as our personal lives. Conscious behavior, mindfulness, and compassion aren't discussed or taught, and for the most part are nonexistent ideas in this workplace ecosystem.

What if we changed that? What if we started prioritizing emotional intelligence, conscious behavior, mindfulness, and compassion as traits in organizational leaders? What if we redefined leadership, made it more aspirational—bigger than any one organization, product, service, or brand?

Let's redefine leadership as the potential of a system to actually sense and shape the future as it emerges. This would translate into awareness-based leadership that is fundamentally based on realigning both individual and collective attention and intention.

Leaders have access to power. There is an energy and a currency to that power, and leaders have the capacity to manage that power. Just like we all learned in elementary school, that energy can be positive or negative. Can you imagine the potential impact if every leader leveraged that currency of power for good, for the benefit of each employee? If they could harness that energy for each employee, by empowering them, engaging them in a company's mission, vision, and values—what an energetic powerhouse they could create by developing an aligned workforce. That positive energetic power would turn to profit, the ultimate goal for any successful business, and the added bonus to that success would be the creation of an engaged workplace.

IN MY CAREER across the healthcare landscape, I have developed countless engagement protocols to help patients succeed in their respective healing journey. These protocols or processes leverage education, digital tools, and other support mechanisms to help patients take their medication on time, or monitor their blood pressure, or understand why their glucose levels need to stay at a certain level. While providing these tools and educational soundbites, the ultimate goal was always to empower these patients to take a more conscious and aligned approach to their own healthcare and to be aware that every decision they make will impact how they feel that day—and ultimately their treatment journey.

Engaged is an interesting word not commonly used in the workplace. It's usually defined as either being "busy" or "occupied" or "having a formal agreement to marry." Most of us are familiar with the implications of the latter definition. What if we repurpose this word as I propose here?

After years of observing my program's success I've realized that we can all benefit from engagement protocols, and across various aspects of our lives. I suggest redefining engagement to mean the conscious participation in an activity with mindful and purposeful thoughts, actions, and energy. In the ecosystem of the workplace, these would create paths and protocols for how managers, leaders, and even CEOs interact with their teams. Conversely they would affect how employees conduct themselves in completing their respective duties and interacting with other team members.

The fundamentals of this engagement protocol are quite easy. The E's (or "ease" to help you remember) of Engagement method is simple, effective, and easy to rollout in any organization. Its goal is to leverage the focus, drive, determination, and combined coherence of a workforce to help achieve corporate goals.

We've already hit upon the first 'E'—**Energy, the power of leadership as a currency.** Leadership can wield this currency for the betterment of their teams and this begins with a certain level of compassion that must by embodied by the leader. Compassion is empathy—identifying with another's feelings and emotions—in action. Can you imagine if the majority of business leaders actively practiced compassion in the execution of their daily roles? If a leader truly takes the time to understand the potential of his or her position—to embrace being a leader, to leverage their emotional intelligence, to strive to be of service—that energy can only yield positive results.

The next step, the second 'E', is Education. Leaders and C-suite members are always tasked with corporate goals—whether revenue targets, membership growth, or other metrics selected from above. These metrics are selected to gauge the success of the company and are typically only shared at executive level. This brings a degree of stress, and therefore stressful energy, to any given leadership team.

But, what if these corporate goals and targets were presented to employees in simplified and digestible soundbites? What if leadership power was converted to communication? By sharing these goals a level of trust is established between leadership and the workforce. That trust can be further fostered by additional levels of communication, i.e. by consistent sharing of the company's mission and values.

Embodiment is our third 'E'; leaders must practice what they preach and lead by example. Let's pause for a minute. Imagine having a captive audience of employees and taking the time to share heart-based stories or case studies that highlight the corporate mission and values at work in the community. These could be stories of healing, of overcoming adversity, or even highlights from a company-wide volunteer day. By embracing, reinforcing, and embodying organizational values, leaders drive up their energetic currency. This elicits an expanse of heart-centered emotion. That level of heart-focused energy in a collective group represents a powerful force and has an even greater potential impact than a group of factory workers on an assembly line (the base from which our current workday was established). **As you may have guessed, 'Eliciting Emotion' represent our fourth 'E'.**

The HeartMath Institute has helped validate the existence of this heart-brain power with multiple studies. By understanding health heart rhythms and frequencies, and correlating these waves with certain activities and emotions, an ideal frequency can be established that represents the heart-brain alignment.[1] This alignment can then be measured and correlated to the activities and coordinated sensory impulses that caused them. The data from these efforts have highlighted that higher cognitive function, more positive feelings, and greater emotional balance can all be garnered from an aligned heart-brain connection.[2] Returning to our captive audience scenario, the ability to create and then harness that heart-focused energy creates a new potential power, a new energy source, that can be tapped into.

Now that you have a captive audience with aligned energy, what next? What if you coupled these feel-good stories and emotions with strategic goals and objectives—converted that group's heart coherence into aligned energy and plans of action for addressing a specific quarter's goals? The creative force would then be available to the leadership team as the employees collectively embrace production or revenue goals while embodying the energy of being aligned, as a group, in supporting the corporate mission and values.

While I know many organizations leverage the Town Hall system, which is the essence of what's described above, the biggest mistake that companies can make is holding Town Halls only to check the box. How many of us have sat through these events and ultimately realized that the leadership is out of touch and their comments are completely off-base? In order to create the energy above, leadership must embody a unique blend of emotional intelligence, compassion, and dedication—the awareness-based leadership defined earlier. And this engagement doesn't have to be through a town hall. There are multiple other ways to engage with employees such as acknowledging birthdays, work anniversaries, or special family moments. The essence is embodying the mindset of a compassionate leader and letting that energy drive the actions and engagement with the employees in meaningful and sustainable ways.

The energetic exchange between leader and employees should flow both ways, the proverbial give and take. If leaders use their compassion to not only motivate and enlist their employees' drive and focus in working toward corporate goals, they must also strive to employ methodologies to empower their workforce as human beings. These can include employee health and wellness benefits, the ability to truly take time off (many of us have worked in roles where taking PTO was just an exercise and we would work as needed), support mechanisms (legal help, mental health benefits), and creating a social environment or community. While this was probably prioritized to a greater degree pre-Covid, when most of us worked in offices, this sense of community is still important to create. It's estimated that employees typically spend 90,000 hours at work over their lifetime—about one-third of their lives.[3] **Enabled and Empowered Employees, our fifth 'E',** creates an energized workforce that then drives forward revenue and production or service goals. Investing in establishing a sense of community for that powerhouse of a workforce will continue to foster an environment of empowerment and support—long after the Town Hall, community event, or other engagement activity has passed.

Transforming the business ecosystem is about understanding the currency of power. Awareness-based leadership is a new concept that actively engages and leverages that power and consists of three priorities: being present, showing compassion, and being collaborative. Being present may seem daunting, but it simply means paying attention to where my attention, as a leader, goes. Here are some key questions that you can use to help realign and focus this presence:

1. Am I actively listening? Or actively talking (to be heard)?
2. Am I taking power, or using power?
3. Am I empowering others?

The critical point here is that being present doesn't mean you have to solve anyone's problems. It is simply your acknowledgement of their given situation or comment in real time. Showing compassion is relatively self-explanatory. As we noted earlier, empathy is the ability to understand another individual's feelings or emotions. Compassion is the action of that understanding, having a mindset of wishing the best for others, and the courage-desire to alleviate suffering or to help. Finally, collaboration is a function of integrating the above components of awareness-based leadership while partnering with employees to be more effective, productive, and profitable while keeping corporate entropy systems—like office politics—low. In other words, to maximize gains, one must minimize the drains.

I know I would have benefitted from such a leader over the last eighteen years. I also would have benefitted from:

- A workplace where my drive, focus, and performance were fostered
- An organization where my health and wellness were prioritized
- A leadership team that actually listened and addressed employee concerns
- A leadership team that shared, for instance, that because of reduced profits they planned on pausing 401K contributions instead of making layoffs

That level of compassion, that level of effort, that level of consideration, is what is needed from awareness-based leaders.

Much evidence exists to highlight the positive aspects of compassionate leaders: improved employee productivity, retention, and morale; higher customer engagement; innovation; service quality; financial performance; and the always undervalued adaptability to change.[4] Interestingly, many leaders struggle with whether they should lead with empathy—which can lead to fatigue —or lead with compassion, which improves resilience and strategic direction. Furthermore, many leaders may understand the power of compassion but don't know how to integrate it into their leadership style.

Awareness-based leadership calls for a new breed of leaders— those who are willing to look within and without simultaneously. Leaders with a level of emotional intelligence, presence, transparency, clarity, trust, and compassion, who will shift the current business ecosystem. This next-gen leadership will not only optimize our workplaces but also create positive energetics that support production, profit, and ultimately, success.

Erem Latif

ErEM LATIF is a visionary healthcare executive with twenty years' success in behavioral health and neuroscience marketing. Having spent most of her career developing engagement protocols for patients, Latif shares an innovative engagement methodology to foster compassionate leadership, employee wellness, and corporate success. Latif has a BS in Biology (Emory University), MS in Biomedical Science (Georgetown University), and an MBA in healthcare management (Florida Institute of Technology).

FOURTEEN

All Rise

Karin Frosio

I'd finally taken the first step towards moving outside of my immense personal grief. It was the summer of 2007, and I was still reeling from the birth and death (both occurred on the same day) of our full-term daughter, Marisa. I sat alone at the back of the sanctuary, wallowing in self-pity. Just like the Dead Sea with no life and at the lowest point on earth, I too was at the lowest point in my life with nothing left to give.

My husband and I were both hurting. We had so many unanswered questions. Neither of us knew how best to support the other and at any given time we seemed to have opposite needs. The large church made it easy for me to slip in and out without having to connect with anyone; just what I wanted. I had put up a shell around myself, limiting emotions and interactions so I could mask the pain and attempt to function normally amid my immense loss.

Music has always opened my heart and soul. That day was no different. As music played and words were sung, my emotions were front and center. I remember looking around at the back of all the heads and saying to myself, "Here I am, and not one person knows or understands the pain I'm feeling."

But a split second later another thought came through like a lightning bolt. It was as if God said, "Do you know what *that* person is going through? Or that one?"

As I looked around I was awestruck as I realized that no, I didn't know what anyone else was going through: a divorce, a terminal illness, the death of a loved one perhaps.

I was part of the walking wounded without even realizing it. The term is typically used in medical triage. An injury may not be noticeable at first, so the walking wounded are deemed capable. But in a triage or first aid setting they often wait for the more serious needs of others to be attended, even if they're in a significant amount of pain or brokenness. Likewise, we often have no idea which hurt, injuries, or needs may be unseen in those we come across daily.

This new visceral awareness continued to expand my heart. I wasn't alone. Every single person, in and outside of work, was similarly the walking wounded. Despite our emotional or psychological scars from life's experiences, so often unknown to others, we continue functioning to meet daily demands and the needs of others. It lightened my load to realize that like me, everyone needs grace and compassion. In the years since, I've reflected on this "Aha!" moment and have seen my perception of, and reaction to, others completely altered.

MY EMOTIONS DIDN'T NECESSARILY CHANGE OVERNIGHT. I've often heard that you have to "feel it to heal it." You have to fully process an emotion to move through it. I was still prone to unanticipated responses to certain stimuli that reopened the wound, but my perspective did take on a new sense of compassion, not just for myself, but for others. This insight continues to weave its way into every personal and professional interaction and steers my leadership style.

We could have easily, and maybe even justifiably, placed the blame for our loss on various individuals in the doctor's office. Placing blame would have united me and my husband. It would have felt good in so many ways to have someone pay a price. But placing blame wouldn't change the past. It would only infect the present with a continued negative focus and could even sabotage the future. It's hard to image how different life would be now if my focus had stayed tied up in blame, lawsuits, and ruining others' lives and reputations.

It's hard to believe that such a devastating event forced positive change—helping me to connect better with others and to learn to lead with compassion. One of the biggest changes was becoming mindful of assumptions. In 2007 I'd assumed everyone else that day was just fine. I was the only one hurting and no one knew it. That was a wrong assumption, one of many I now see I can err towards daily.

For starters, consider how myopic each of us tend to be. We typically focus on our own viewpoint, concern, or personal experiences, and believe this to be sufficient. It's easy to criticize if we are only considering the facts from our perspective. Stopping this assumption involves opening ourselves up to a more inclusive view.

As a young child, there was a bulletin board on the kitchen wall behind the table where we ate our meals. Daily I saw one saying listed as an Indian Proverb: "Don't criticize your brother until you've walked a mile in his moccasins." (I've since learned this heartfelt concept may have originally come from Mary T. Lathrop's 1895 poem, "Judge Softly" or "Walk a Mile in His Moccasins.")

I went on to share this saying through the years, repeating it when first meeting with teams I'd be leading. It helped set the tone for my hope and expectation that we all assume the best of each other, whether it be colleagues, customers, or leaders, while we learn more about each other's perspective and situation. This type of shift in perspective allows us to see the complexities of situations and the challenges others face, thereby fostering compassion.

To lead with compassion it's essential that we each become aware of the unconscious, default assumptions that we make daily, and that we're mindful of choosing a more compassionate alternative. Consider a few assumptions and their results:

- Assumptions about what customers want before understanding their unique situations, only to develop products, services, or solutions that don't meet their needs.
- Assumptions about individual/team needs. If you are in an office setting, consider following Toyota's lead and make time for regular Gemba Walks around your workplace to observe the environment, improve communication, get to know employees, proactively spot potential issues, and boost collaboration. If your team is remote, this can be accomplished by scheduled virtual one-on-one video meetings with your direct reports, and Skip-Level meetings with those that don't report directly to you.
- The forever assumption, believing since it's always been this way, it always will be this way, is dangerous and stifling.
- Assuming we know the motives of others has pitfalls. After our loss, I assumed some dear friends just didn't care when they didn't reach out. I later learned they were at such a loss for how to respond, that they just didn't. Preconceived notions cloud our judgement. Misinterpreting someone's intentions leads to misunderstandings and can unnecessarily escalate situations. Assuming the motives of others can foster an environment of mistrust rather than open communication.
- Assuming one has to always appear strong can not only lead to emotional distress but hinder personal growth. Have you created any barriers in your quest to always appear competent that keep you walled off from truly connecting with others?

I've even made the mistake of assuming others know that they are appreciated. S. Truett Cathy, the Founder of Chik-Fil-A, is credited with saying, "How do you identify someone who needs encouragement? That person is breathing."[1] We should seize every opportunity to offer encouragement and show our appreciation of others.

Assume, instead, that everyone needs encouragement. I encourage you to make a list of assumptions you are prone to utilizing that may not be serving you well in leading with compassion, so that you can also continue growing in this area.

ASSUMPTIONS not only play a crucial role in how we perceive and respond to situations, they can also significantly affect how we experience and express vulnerabilities. By examining our assumptions, we can foster a more accepting environment for diversity and vulnerability and allow for deeper connections and personal development.

But it's more than recognizing that we are all part of the walking wounded and all need encouragement. We don't know what form of encouragement is best for different people. Those around us aren't just suddenly going to open up. Do you know the emotional culture in your sphere of influence? Once we know more about what others are going through, we can better support them and help remove obstacles.

It can be scary to open yourself up. We like to look as though we have it all together. But what are you modeling? Isolation? Every man for himself? Whether exacerbated by cultural gaps, remote work, fragmented structures, over-reliance on digital interactions, global issues, social isolation, or emotional disconnection—your daily intentional efforts to be more vulnerable will foster connection and community.

What we say or do is as important as what we don't say or do. You can't, and shouldn't, try to do everything on your own. Not only is it OK to ask for help, but by not doing so you are depriving others of the chance to connect and grow. You may also miss out on new perspectives that could truly enhance your project or situation. What are you refraining from sharing?

Even otters know the importance of vulnerability. I recently learned that when female otters sleep, they hold hands. This tactic, called rafting, keeps them from drifting away from each other and enables them to share body heat to stay warm and conserve energy. Some insights from the otters:

- **Mutual support**. Interdependence, connection, and collaboration is essential, and often leads to greater achievements and resilience against challenges as we share burdens and joys. For humans, striking a balance between personal autonomy and nurturing relationships is crucial.
- **Ask for help**. We've all heard that the only stupid question is the one you don't ask. Are you creating an environment where it's safe to ask for help? Shared responsibilities also provide a safety net for projects and room for personal growth. Does your team see you prioritizing self-care, making time for a walk during lunch, scheduling and utilizing your PTO benefits? Have you encouraged them to speak up if there is a problem with a proposed deadline? If a deadline is going to negatively impact someone's life because of a conflict I don't know about, I want to hear about it and explore options together. In fact, leave scheduled wiggle room, so that you have flexibility in your schedule and projects.
- **Create a safe space.** Otters holding hands create strength from vulnerability and a safe place for all. Is your team encouraged to reach out to someone they trust? In human relationships, emotional safety strengthens bonds and fosters trust.

SMALL CHANGES MAY SEEM inconsequential in the moment, but they can significantly impact your life and all those in your circle of influence. Consider weaving micro-moments of mindfulness into your day to expand your ability to lead with compassion. Here's a few to get you started:

- **Create a culture of care.** Each of us can nurture our ability to have an extra measure of grace for others' humanity. We're not called to be perfect, we're called to be human. Being human, by its very nature means not being perfect. Together our unique puzzle pieces of imperfections can create a beautiful, impactful force.
- **Breathe before you start any new interaction.** Consider your intention of that connection.
- **Notice how you walk into a room.** Are you smiling and engaged, or already multi-tasking? Make time first for connection before jumping headfirst into an agenda.
- **Look into the eyes of the person in front of you.** Don't let yourself become distracted by others, your computer, your phone, etc.
- **Read emails at least two times and breathe.** Consider your tone and response instead of quickly sending off a reply you may regret later.

Learning to lead with compassion is sacred work. No matter what type of life you lead or position you hold, you are impacting the lives of others and leading by example. Each interaction (or lack thereof) has a positive or negative effect. Our life experiences and gifts aren't just for us. They are for one another. Don't hide them under a bushel. Small purposeful steps each day will enhance your journey toward being your best for the world, rather than being the best in the world. Focus on compassionate daily habits and the results will take care of themselves.

Take care of yourself, take care of others, and together, you can take care of business.

Karin Frosio

KARIN FROSIO, founder of Revive Joy, believes well-being is the gateway to driving desired results and is committed to promoting a culture of compassion within and beyond the workplace. Building on over thirty years of inspirational leadership experience, Revive Joy empowers individuals and transforms teams/organizations with innovative strategies and workshops to maximize performance and elevate quality of life. Karin celebrates life in Florida, where she resides with her husband.

FIFTEEN

Will You Recognize It When You See It?

Meenu Datta

Almost fourteen years ago I was hired as a consultant for a time-bound project to build a center of excellence. I had done similar work before and felt at home right away after joining the organization. Our team was making great progress and soon we were going to deliver our first project using the new processes and workflows. There was an exciting yet nerve-wracking buzz surrounding us, as the project we were shifting to the new process was a part of a program generating over three billion dollars annually.

At home, life was equally demanding. My toddler had not yet started to sleep through the night and I had been feeling like a zombie for over a year, so sleep-deprived was I. As if that was not enough, just two days before my birthday, a comical yet tragic event occurred when I injured my back at a child's birthday party. I bent down to greet the birthday girl and something snapped in my back, leaving me immobile in that exact pose. I couldn't move a step ahead or back, or stand straight. We left the party early and I took some painkillers and remember sleeping through almost the entire weekend including my birthday.

On Monday, I was in the office, making my way slowly to the conference room in the morning when my manager approached me with a look of concern.

"What happened?" he asked.

Before I could stop and turn slowly one step at a time, he was standing beside me with an expression that was a mix of curiosity, confusion, and concern. I explained briefly, expecting the focus to quickly turn to the meeting about the upcoming delivery.

"What are you doing here?" he went on to ask.

It felt like a rhetorical question. Confused, I responded with the obvious: "We have our first delivery in two weeks. You know how everyone feels about the changes we're making. Nothing could..."

I couldn't finish my sentence to emphasize the urgency, and he seemed oblivious.

"Let's talk after the meeting," he said.

The conversation I had with him after the meeting was a turning point for me. It hadn't occurred to me that I could request an alternate work setting two weeks before a major delivery as a consultant! I was focused on advocating for the project but he assured me I could continue working from home to recover faster, and come back to the office when I could walk faster than my toddler. This was the first time I saw compassionate leadership at play, and where I was least expecting it too: in a workplace. My manager's compassion went beyond feeling my pain and understanding what I was going through. His genuine concern and desire to help brought self-awareness and compassion into my life in a way that made me completely rethink my understanding of leadership.

I realized for the first time that I was kinder to others than to myself. I always made logical and responsible decisions without considering my own needs. I hadn't seen myself as part of the equation and focused only on the immediate tasks that I didn't want to fall short on. My manager's compassionate decision revealed a new leadership style that looked beyond immediate objectives to genuinely caring for team members.

As I navigated my recovery, I reflected on this experience and on my previous neglect of self-compassion. I had been so consumed with protecting my work that I ignored my own health and realized that I had done that multiple times in the past. It felt like I had been moving through work in a trance, and this realization was a wake-up call. My manager's empathy and support showed me that I wasn't alone in dealing with my injury; it was a challenge that we could tackle together.

IN THE WEEKS and months that followed, I developed a habit of reflection. In doing so I gained a deeper understanding of how much I had underestimated my own pain and situation and a deeper appreciation of what my manager had done for me. He had taught me a lifelong lesson. I had been trying to ignore my pain and had avoided acknowledging it, yet he had grasped my struggles better than I had myself. This incident was the beginning of my journey into self-care and setting boundaries. It reshaped how I viewed leadership and increased my ability to entrust my team with challenges in my absence. It also boosted my confidence in remote work, long before remote work became common during COVID.

Before this incident, I had a particular image of compassionate people: gentle, soft-spoken, patient, and always eager to help. But this experience revealed the multifaceted nature of compassion. I had been narrowing it down to only a few traits. This realization sparked my curiosity and mindfulness around compassion's many expressions. As a young professional or even as a student, what once seemed like strictness from teachers or bosses began to reveal themselves as acts of compassion, intended for my growth even if not explicitly stated. The tough love they showed in helping me set boundaries and instill discipline was a form of compassion. My view shifted from thinking, *He was really strict, but I learned a lot by working with him*—to realizing, *He cared deeply and helped me grow.*

I have always valued direct and honest feedback because I believe in continually improving myself. There are some strengths and areas of growth that others can see more clearly than we do. I realized that it was easy to revert back to autopilot, forgetting the lessons learned about setting boundaries and self-care. So I started actively seeking feedback at work and in personal relationships. I was allowing myself to reflect more often and connect the dots across different phases of my life. I was seeing the compassion I had previously overlooked.

EARLY IN MY CAREER, I worked with managers who either allowed me to make mistakes and learn from them, or who were overly cautious and prevented any errors. I came to see the former approach as an act of compassion that facilitated growth through experience. It felt like compassion was suddenly everywhere around me and I wondered what had changed. It's like when you decide to buy a particular car model or color, and suddenly you see it everywhere. I realized that my newfound ability to see compassion was because I had chosen to build more self-compassion. Having compassion within me helped me to see it around me.

Since that experience almost a decade and a half ago, I have taken every opportunity to learn more about the role of self-awareness and compassion in our lives, often discussing their presence—or absence—in the workplace.

I have encountered many beliefs, principles, misconceptions, and myths around compassion. Some see compassion as weak or inefficient. One executive thought it was a feminine trait. When I heard "feminine" I thought he implied "weakness", thanks to past male bosses. But this executive saw it as a natural gift for women and a challenge for men. His perception was influenced by his two sisters, both executives, who made people-centered decisions more easily than he did. This insight deepened my empathy for those who viewed compassion as an inherently feminine trait. Two things happened because of this discussion: we both came to the conclusion that empathy, compassion, and decision-making are not tied to gender—and it inspired me to advocate for compassion as a leadership skill that like any other skill can be cultivated in anyone irrespective of gender. I shared some women-led initiatives at work and encouraged this executive to participate to understand how compassion can coexist with effective results. It's not an either/or scenario. Compassion can drive better and faster outcomes.

Compassion needs to be understood as a skill without putting it in boxes like masculine versus feminine, strong versus weak, inherent versus cultivated. Just as empathy and compassion teach us to not be judgmental, we need to understand these traits without judging or putting labels on them. We'll then see that compassion comes in many forms, beyond traditional gender roles or expectations. It's all around us, often in unexpected places. We see it in tough love from mentors and leaders or the support of friends and colleagues. We see it when we allow our feelings without judging them and when we let go of negative emotions. We generate it in respectfully challenging others to grow beyond their self-imposed limits and in setting healthy boundaries. We embody it through advocacy, intervention, and self-care.

You may already practice compassionate leadership without realizing it, for you are a compassionate leader when you:

- Hold your team accountable for their actions and behaviors to help them grow
- Address a conflict with a peer, team member, or manager directly, even when it's uncomfortable
- Trust your team to do their job and allow them to continue their process of reaching the solution
- Fight to get funds, tools, or headcount to help improve your team's working conditions
- Share difficult decisions honestly and transparently with your team instead of keeping the decisions from them to protect them
- Take care of yourself and set boundaries and encourage the same for your team
- Step away to help your team learn and experiment and bring solutions you can't see

- Step up to help and support your team in challenging times
- Give a chance to someone with great potential instead of giving it to an obvious choice

Sometimes people may not understand your actions. Sharing the why behind a decision is an act of compassion because you are helping push the boundaries of someone's worldview.

To recognize where we can act with compassion we can:

1. Look for the genuine intention behind someone's actions
2. Seek to understand if help addresses root causes and not just symptoms
3. Consider long-term benefits, even when short-term gains aren't obvious

These three steps have become my guide. They help me avoid knee-jerk reactions to well-meaning support, to practice patience and forgiveness, and to expand my acceptance of different situations. By pausing to reflect on these points I've learned to be more mindful of the compassion around me and this has deepened my understanding and improved my relationships.

Embracing compassion can really enrich our lives, both personally and professionally. While we might perceive a lack of compassion in many workplaces, there's a growing recognition among leaders that compassion is not just a nice-to-have, but a powerful tool for achieving business goals. More leaders are realizing that combining financial ambition with a compassionate culture isn't contradictory, it's transformative. This powerful mix of heart and hustle can elevate companies from good to great, driving both employee satisfaction and financial growth. Leaders need to see beyond survival mode or short-term gains to enjoy the benefits of leading with compassion.

The other reason for the apparent lack of compassion in some environments may also stem from our own difficulty in recognizing it. To see compassion in the outer world, we must first cultivate it within ourselves. Learning self-compassion unlocks our ability to recognize and appreciate it around us. It creates a positive feedback loop that benefits everyone in the organization. And as more leaders adopt this approach we're likely to see a shift towards more compassionate, and ultimately more successful, workplaces.

Meenu Datta

MEENU DATTA a certified executive and leadership coach, is the founder of MD Coaching and Consulting. With over twenty years of tech experience leading transformation initiatives for Fortune 500 companies, she now focuses on empowering leaders by nurturing their inner world to unlock their immense potential. Her dedication lies in creating sustainable change through a coaching culture. Residing in North Carolina, she enjoys the tranquility of nature with her family.

SIXTEEN

The Path Less Travelled: Opening up to Others

Vincent Smith

O h, shit.
    That was my first thought, and my second, and maybe my third.

I had just moved from a small tech company of about 4,500 people to a very big one of 120,000. A few months on the job and I was handed a critical compliance project from the board of directors—which had already failed twice before and with seasoned internal staff.

A well-established company-wide template and process had already been used twice, had failed both times, and the Program Managers had to move on after failing. What was the barrier— why wasn't standard practice working and how was I going to keep my job!?

Finding myself in the middle of an irreconcilable challenge was pretty common for me.

Let's rewind to the beginning.

STRESS, panic, fear, endless ruminating, trying to keep track of every task, every deadline, trying to anticipate the next problem, having nightmares about every little detail, waking before the alarm anticipating the next deadline to hit. All to create safety and predictability through control and brute force.

This was my life as a tech program manager.

I was good at organizing and coordinating and I was overwhelmed most of the time. Constant change and endless pressure. Ultimately fear drove me. Fear of failure, fear of dropping the ball, fear of losing my job, fear of not being able to find a new one, fear of failing my family in the super-expensive Bay Area.

I was living a bit of a double life but didn't realize it at the time. I started my career as an engineer but found my place working with people, looking beneath the surface, listening closely and really understanding what was going on for them. I was always best at working through the people parts of the program, bringing them together toward a shared goal. But tech was all about data, deadlines, and constant change. My greatest strength wasn't understood or rewarded.

As I continued to explore my affinity for people I found myself in a program for coach training. I was excited, I got this, I work with people every day—what could go wrong?

Yikes! The shock and vulnerability.

First class, first five minutes of a three-day intensive on a cool October Friday, I found myself in a room full of strangers in the middle of an icebreaker.

The two trainers were back-to-back in the center of the room, the twenty-five students in a circle around them. The trainers explained the process. They will slowly spin in the center while they call on students to coach them. The trainer will call on students randomly and spontaneously, and the new student will need to pick up the coaching session where it left off.

Let me lay this out for you more clearly. I had survived my career by relentlessly preparing, anticipating everything and never showing up to a meeting without knowing all the answers in advance. And I lean introverted. Now I'm standing in a circle of strangers, expected to coach the trainers on demand, on whatever they're talking about. No prep, no thought, no practice, no experience. It was terrifying.

Holy crap. It was intense. I wanted to run out of the room. It took all my strength to stay and participate through to the end. And that was only the start. I still had six hours and thirty minutes left in day one of three.

The intensity kept coming: different types of activities and the training model was extremely experiential (read: vulnerable). I wanted to take notes; I wasn't allowed. I wanted to understand the agenda and prepare; no agenda available. Everything was spontaneous. I was exhausted by the end of the day and wasn't sure I wanted to come back for the next day's torture. I seriously questioned if I could keep doing this. It was the exact opposite of everything I was doing to protect myself in my career.

I made it back the next morning, shaken and anxious, but I dove in again. The second day was a little easier, a little less shocking, but still I ended up completely exhausted. Every piece of armor was being stripped away violently.

On the third and final day of the class—another huge challenge —everyone lined up until there was a line across the middle of the floor dividing the room. Each person was required to share a vulnerable truth that was new to the class, then leap over the line while everyone watched. A bit like a trust fall but much more intense. My panic level was through the roof. I was a very private person. I didn't share personal things with the outside world. My mind was racing: what am I going to say, to strangers!? I could fake it and share something that wasn't vulnerable, that seemed like a really good idea right about now—or I could go all in, "do the work" and share something I didn't want anyone to know. The first, then the second and third person leaped over the line. Some made it easily, some really struggled. I knew it was illogical to feel panic, but damn. Mind racing, what am I going to say? There's no out, everyone who leaped over before me had turned around and was looking right at me. Okay, great, now I have an engaged audience too...

Okay, okay, wait a minute, slow down, I'm thinking. *I'm not ready.*

There was no time to think, but it wasn't about thinking, it was about being in the moment, trusting others, being vulnerable, and blurting something out. This was not at all how I had been living my life.

I'm at the line, everyone looking at me and still I haven't come up with something safe.

"I'm in love with someone," I blurted out then leaped over the line.

There's quiet, then applause, my heart skipped a beat, but I survived.

Then my brain caught up with what I had just said. *Wait, what, in public?*

It was an overwhelming moment. I had just said, out loud, something I hadn't really realized or acknowledged before that moment, something I hadn't shared with anyone. And I just shared it with a room full of strangers.

It took me a minute; I drifted into the back of the room. I was still standing; I was still safe, and I was still shaking from the intensity. After the activity a few people came over to encourage me. I realized in that moment that I had been safe, that there was compassion in the room, and that the exercise, as stressful and vulnerable as it was, helped me trust and lean into those around me.

I survived the first course, it started a transformation within me, in how I saw myself, how I experienced the world and engaged the people around me.

YEARS PASSED and I continued the coaching course series. The courses continued to be intense, and I continued to feel vulnerable, but now there was more trust and, at times, exhilaration from connecting deeper with myself and others. I continued to lean in and practice letting go of the armor I was carrying. I continued to lean into the people part of work, continued to practice listening closely, seeking to understanding, partnering and engaging with compassion.

Fast forward to that new job.

Shit's about to get real. The critical program was global, with eighteen senior leaders around the world, each head of their operations, the same eighteen that had been part of the two prior failed attempts.

They knew the template, the process, and the business far better than I did. I had 6 months to accomplish all the program goals, to change the company's operations and how customers interacted with them—with a VP and the board of directors watching over everything. No pressure.

I was on fire, scrambling, the clock was ticking. I was on autopilot. I was trying to ramp up on everything while trying not to let overwhelm paralyze me.

I kicked off meetings, following the process exactly. I did everything I could to bring people together, I had morning and evening meetings to accommodate time zones around the globe. I over-communicated, created clear documentation, purpose, plan and tasks. My job was on the line, I wasn't leaving anything to chance. Firefighting like this was exactly why I had all the armor in the past.

I was a machine, driving the process forward. Everyone showed up for the meetings, and responded to emails, they knew the drill, it was part of the culture, it wasn't optional. A few weeks past, I noticed that despite apparent participation we weren't making progress.

Uh oh.

Is this what happened to the prior program managers? Is this why the program had failed twice before? What's going on? Why aren't we moving forward? Instructions are clear, tasks are clear, everyone is in the room—so what was I missing?

As I stepped back a bit, letting go of my death grip on the task list and timeline, and reminded myself to lean into the people, the team and dynamics, I began to see subtle distractions. A random comment here, indecision there, ambiguous concerns voiced after a decision was finalized. I started to realize there was unspoken friction in the team. The problem was never the template or process, it was that the people weren't feeling seen and safe.

The clock is ticking, the timeline is nearly impossible, and people on the team aren't bought in.

I kept moving forward, but now I was much more focused on figuring out where the people really stood. I began to see patterns. In particular there seemed to be a couple of senior leaders indirectly and subtly challenging different parts of the project. Theirs were more like reactions or impulses than intent. Decision time for me. I could escalate and force progress or I could suspend judgement and seek to understand what was really going on for each of them.

The decision was simple. Before my coaching courses and efforts to be more present, the standard process would have been to escalate. It was the most direct and efficient action, but it can be destructive. This time I was going to do it differently. Although pressure was high and untangling the people part of the project wasn't technically part of my scope, I wanted to collaborate, not escalate.

Focusing on these two leaders, I began to realize that this entire program had upended the normal company culture. Everyone on the team went from autonomous empowered leaders in control of their own domain, to stakeholders being told what to do by their superiors and led by me—the most junior person on the team. They had lost most of their authority. They had lost their sense of agency. They were vulnerable and it was spilling into the team.

Ah, okay, now I get it. The world around them had changed and nobody checked in with them. It was assumed they were on-board. It was subtle, people hadn't reacted immediately, there was no direct action against the program. Now the random questions and distractions made sense. They were each trying to find ways to assert themselves and regain their sense of identity and control. Now I understood why the template and process didn't solve the problem. I needed to find a way to resolve their vulnerability while continuing with the program.

I began meeting with the key leaders one on one, getting a read on where they were at, seeking to understand what they needed and what I could do to create safety for them. For one of them, the recognition through dedicated one on ones and advance notice of topics and decisions, solved the problem. For the other, I found that data was his passion and his identity, and realized another change in the normal operating procedure. This program wasn't using his team for the data, it was using a third party. He didn't know the team, didn't know how they were extracting and managing the data, and didn't trust it. He needed to be actively involved. He needed to supervise the data portion of the program or we'd never receive his crucial engagement and support. I was able to negotiate with the third party to insert him into a leadership role. He moved from challenging every piece of data in the program to being the data champion on the team.

It was a six-month fire, the third attempt. We got it across the line, on time, and on budget.

I realized that without the people, nothing can be accomplished. The best templates, processes, and culture in the world can't deliver results if people don't come first.

Vincent Smith

VINCENT SMITH is the founder of Quantum Leap Coaching, a professional coaching and mentoring organization focused on working with individuals through a uniquely compassionate, intuition-based approach to cultivate and accelerate self-awareness, overcome vulnerabilities, build resilience, and develop authenticity. He combines ten years' experience as a certified coach with twenty-five years as a business leader at Fortune 500 companies, where he successfully brings people together to solve novel personal and organizational challenges.

The Purpose in Witnessing

If we gain the ability to look into ourselves with honesty, compassion, and with unclouded vision, we can identify the ways we need to take care of ourselves. We can see the areas of self formerly hidden in the dark. [1]

Gabor Maté

SEVENTEEN

Following the Call: A Story of Priorities, Presence, and Heartfelt Choices

Ashanti Branch

I t was supposed to be a straightforward trip back home from Nashville. I had attended a conference and my mind was already racing with the tasks I needed to complete once I landed. I was behind on writing a critical chapter for a book project—something I had committed to months earlier. The manuscript was due the next day and I had only a few precious hours left to pull it together. I was determined to finish it. The plan was simple: drop off my bags, head to a café, crank out a solid five hours of writing to complete the first draft.

But things didn't go as planned.

As the plane took off I received a text message from a young man I mentor. His words hit me hard.

"I'm not doing well right now. I'm in my head."

Immediately my mind started spinning. I've seen this kind of message before—enough to know that it isn't something you can brush off. These words often carry the weight of things unspoken: anxiety, depression, or worse. Part of me thought, *I don't have time for this right now. I've got this book chapter to write.* Another part of me knew I had to respond. These moments are never easy, and this young man was reaching out for a reason.

As we exchanged texts I quickly realized that typing responses mid-flight wasn't going to cut it. A text message offers only so much connection. I'm not a therapist but I know how to listen. I know how to reflect and ask questions to help someone feel seen and understood. But doing that through text? It felt impossible. Still I kept going—typing, waiting for responses, and trying to provide thoughtful feedback.

And then doubt crept in.

What if I cannot finish my writing in time? I thought. *What if I miss another deadline?* This was not just a book project to me—it was a step toward financial freedom, a chance to take care of my future, and a way to avoid the financial struggles that I have witnessed haunt elders in my life and in my family. I have seen what happens when you don't have the resources you need and I've made a commitment to myself: I will create a life where I do not have to rely on anyone else to survive.

But here I was, caught between two equally urgent priorities— my writing and this young man's cry for help. Or perhaps that comparison was not fully accurate—my future wellbeing and this young man's cry for help. No matter how big I made my personal priorities it did not seem anywhere as important as showing up for this young man. And there was no easy answer.

I know the stakes. In my line of work I've seen too many young people lost to the weight of their challenges. Some have turned to self-harm or substances, and some, tragically, did not make it at all. I carry those losses with me every day, along with the daily reminders of the way that my brother's substance abuse and mental health challenges have affected my own life. I've wrestled with guilt in the past—wondering if there was more I could have done.

So what do you do in a moment like this?

Do you stick to your goals and hope someone else steps in? Or do you answer the call, knowing it could mean sacrificing your own ambitions?

Choosing presence over productivity

When I landed, the messages had slowed. I rushed home, washed my face, and packed my bag for the café. Just as I was about to head out I got another text—a picture of a sunset.

Something about that image struck me. It seemed peaceful yet out of place. I knew the young man had said he was going for a walk, but something about it didn't sit right. My gut told me not to ignore it. I decided to call him.

When he picked up I could hear train tracks in the background. My heart skipped a beat. Why was he near train tracks? A swirl of stories filled my mind—memories of others I'd lost, moments when I hadn't intervened in time. I didn't know what was really going on but I knew this wasn't something I could dismiss.

I asked him gently, "Would you like to meet up?"

"Yes."

I could feel the weight of his yes, because I knew how hard it is for him to ask for help, and I have told him in the past that I also have a hard time asking for help and it was only recently where I felt like I have people I can reach out to when I need it.

In that moment everything became clear. The book project could wait; whatever he was going through couldn't. I grabbed what I needed, made a quick stop at my office, and met him where he was.

Over the next few hours, we walked, talked, and ran errands together. I asked questions, listened closely, and watched his body language—the subtle shifts in his posture and facial expressions. I didn't have all the answers, but I knew how to be present. And that's what he needed: someone who would show up and walk with him through the storm.

It was a simple decision in some ways but it felt monumental. As we spent time together, I realized that this—being present for others in their moments of need—is when I am at my best. Not when I'm sitting alone, staring at a blank page, trying to force the right words. But when I'm in the moment, responding to the needs of others, drawing from the stories, lessons, and experiences that life has given me.

And by choosing to show up that night, I knew I was also showing up for the eight-year-old version of myself—the boy who didn't know how to ask for help, who kept his pain bottled up and buried inside. This was part of my healing too.

The importance of following the heart's call

This experience reminded me of something essential: Sometimes the most meaningful work we do isn't what we planned—it's what happens when we follow our hearts.

I had every reason to focus on my own goal that night. The chapter I was supposed to write represented more than just words on a page. It was tied to my financial goals, my dreams of independence, and my desire to create a life where I could care for myself and my family without being a burden. But what I learned in that moment is that some opportunities—like being there for someone in crisis—don't come with second chances.

That young man's text was more than just a message. It was an invitation to be present, to listen, and to show up in the way that only I could. And while the book chapter mattered, this mattered more. Today's young people need more than instruction—they need connection. The world they are growing up in is different from the one we knew. They are navigating constant distractions, social pressures, and an addiction to their devices that makes learning even more challenging.

We have to meet others where they are without lowering our expectations. We have to help them see the value in the work they do, even when they resist it. And we have to be patient—not just with others, but with ourselves. In the work that I do with young people, I have recognized that the way we educate and mentor them must evolve. It's not enough to hand them a set of instructions and expect compliance. We need to create spaces where they feel seen, heard, and respected. We need to give them the tools to navigate their emotions and relationships, and we need to model the behaviors we hope to see in them.

In reflecting on all of this, I realized that writing isn't the only way to tell a story.

That night, I was living the story.

I was embodying the message I would later try to put into words: that connection, presence, and compassion are more important than productivity.

The gift of showing up

If there's one thing I've learned from this experience, it's this: our most important work often lies in the moments when we are simply present for others.

Yes, deadlines and goals are important. Yes, it's essential to take care of yourself and honor your commitments. But sometimes life presents us with opportunities that can't wait—opportunities to be the person someone else needs in a critical moment. And when those moments come, we have to be willing to set aside our own plans and follow the call of our hearts.

Each person has so much more going on with them than they actually let people see. And therefore, if we tell ourselves that no one cares, we operate as if trusting is pointless. Because no one is going to get what we really feel, no matter what. Until we build connection with people around us, so that we recognize and realize that we're not alone, that's not going to change.

Not for us, and not for our children.

We don't have to prove or demonstrate anything. That's exhausting.

If we get the chance to take off our mask, we can create our own safety and trust within ourselves first. And then we will recognize the masks of others, and explore the kinds of masks of other people around us. Safety and trust are right at the heart of Maslow's hierarchy of needs because of how big and important they are to who we are—to how we navigate the world. To whether we feel like we can sing when we are happy and cry when we are sad.

It's not easy. I've read the books and heard the speeches about prioritizing your goals and saying no to distractions. And there is wisdom in that. But I also believe that part of living with purpose is knowing when to bend, when to pause, and when to answer the call to be present.

For anyone who finds themself in a similar situation—torn between personal goals and the needs of others—my advice is this: Trust yourself. Trust that the work you are meant to do will unfold in its own time. And trust that being there for someone in need is never wasted time.

The writing will get done. The goals will still be there. But the chance to make a difference in someone's life? That may only come once.

In the end I didn't finish the chapter that night. But I did something far more important: I showed up. And that made all the difference.

This is the heart of the message I want to leave with others: the gift we carry is not just in the work we do, but in the way we show up for others when they need us most. And sometimes the most profound stories aren't the ones we write—they're the ones we live.

Ashanti Branch

ASHANTI BRANCH, founder of The Ever Forward Club, has over twenty years of experience as an educator dedicated to youth mental wellness and educational reform. He is a recipient of the Surgeon General's Medallion, a Fulbright Fellow, and a four-time TEDx speaker, and was featured in the documentary film *The Mask You Live In*. Through the #MillionMaskMovement, Ashanti has engaged with over 80,000 people worldwide, fostering growth through vulnerability and shared connections.

EIGHTEEN

Seeing Deeply

Wainwright Yu

"She doesn't show up to meetings."

"She says she'll do something and I never hear back."

"She's got brilliant ideas but she doesn't follow through."

These are the words going through my mind as I prepare myself for what I thought was going to be a straightforward performance conversation with an employee, as straightforward as these types of conversations can be.

Amanda enters the virtual meeting room. I say hello. She says hello back, awkwardly. I suspect she knows what I want to talk about. I move the conversation along, sharing in a gentle but determined tone the concerns her peers have about her performance at work. As I speak she looks down at her keyboard and avoids eye contact. I go through a prepared list of examples, each illustrating how she was failing to meet the company's expectations for employees in her role. I did not want to be harsh, I just wanted to be clear. "Clarity is fair," I say to myself. "Clarity is just." I could not see how someone could fail to complete even the most basic tasks at work and not see it coming. This must not be a surprise.

I finished speaking. After some time she looked up.

"I don't know how or if I should tell you this," she says. Her face flush with embarrassment. Her eyes dart about, perhaps seeking some sign that could bring certainty to a mind where there was none. "I have ADHD."

I did not know much about ADHD at the time, but I knew enough to know I needed to learn more. I find out about the accommodations my company offers employees with ADHD. I help this employee sign up for company-sponsored coaching. I extend the time she has to complete the projects in her performance improvement plan. I point her to an employee-facing learning hub that provides tips and tricks for improving executive function. But in the end she continues to struggle and eventually leaves the company. It felt like stopping a moving train. We put the brakes on too late. Collision was inevitable.

PAPERS FLY out the door onto the damp grass in the front yard. A child stumbles onto the porch.

"You can't come back in until you finish your work," I shout and slam the door.

What is 3+2? 5. What is 12+7? 19. What is 21-6? 15. "It's not that hard!" I think to myself, furious. It had been three hours since my son started his math facts homework. There were thirty questions and he had only gotten a handful done.

"It's time for the kiddos to practice independence," I recall hearing his teacher say at the start of the school year. "It's okay if they come in with work that is incorrect. Give them some space to fail and learn."

Well I just wasn't sure she meant turning in a mostly unanswered packet of homework when she suggested creating space for failure. Three hours felt like an awfully long time to be patient and this wasn't our first weekend of homework struggle. Things aren't getting better. I see the 'fail', but where is the 'learn'?

Broken broomsticks, perforated drywall, chairs strewn on the floor. Sound and fury. Pleading, guilt-tripping, and all manner of escalating threats. Week after week, the work got done but at a cost. We arrived at our destination, but we burned all the bridges, pillaged all the towns, slaughtered all the animals, cut down all the trees along the way. In the end we were left with nothing but broken hearts, empty souls, and a really bad taste in our mouths.

It was in these moments of hopelessness that I recall a conversation I had with my son's school principal at a parent-teacher conference a few years earlier.

"Have you considered having him evaluated for ADHD?" she asked.

In the time between this parent-teacher conference and the flying homework incident, I had collected many more facts about ADHD. While I knew a lot more about it in my head, I still felt I knew very little about it in my heart. Dealing with ADHD felt like pushing against a moving train. In the end no matter how hard I try, I get crushed.

As I WALK through our home garden one summer afternoon, I reflect on the many things I've learned about gardening over the years. Lavender needs lots of sun and air but not too much water. Roses, like lavender, love the sun, but they also need a lot of water, so a spot that's just a bit too hot may lead to burnt leaves and quick wilting. Hydrangea are water hungry plants. Place them under part shade and be prepared for frequent watering. They also prefer acidic soil, but I've learned nothing really thrives underneath pine trees and their acid-rich needles.

I've made many mistakes in our garden. On occasion I'd channel my frustration toward "the stupid plant", wishing it would do a better job of growing leaves, producing fruit, or doing whatever else I was hoping for it to do. I would realize of course that the plant had little choice in the matter.

Instead of feeling angry at the plant for not being a better plant, I've learned to accept them as they come, to get to know them as individuals, and to find somewhere in our garden where they might find a home. Failure to thrive—whether you're a plant in a garden, an employee in a workplace, or a child in a classroom—is often rooted in a failure to belong. Our role is to cultivate spaces where everyone and everything can find their place and thrive.

At the heart of compassion is an ability to fully embrace the unique life experiences of those around us. These may have many causes, internal and external. A colleague may have had a recent loss in the family and needs time to grieve. This is an externally driven life circumstance. A colleague with ADHD may be struggling to cope with the demands at work as work cultures shift to a remote, then a hybrid, now back to a mostly in-office environment. This combines both internal and external factors.

I believe that in spite of our flaws we are all fundamentally good, and that our minds and our hearts are naturally oriented towards compassion. However, it is easier to think, feel, and act compassionately towards others with differences you can see. Unfortunately there are many things that set us apart that cannot be seen.

According to research conducted by Jessica Hicksted for her 2023 PhD dissertation at Walden University,[1] 74% of people in the workforce have some form of invisible difference. These invisible differences are diverse in nature and range from sensory differences like sensory-processing disorders, to physical differences like vision impairment, to neurodivergent differences like ADHD.

One of the most insidious barriers to compassion is the assumption that we are or should be the same, that there is some knowable, universal form of good to which we should all aspire.

This assumption is deeply rooted and continually reinforced.

The ancient Greek philosopher Plato argued in his theory of forms that there is a higher order of existence that is divine, unchanging, and flawlessly good, against which all things are but imperfect reproductions. We live Plato's theory of forms in our day-to-day lives at home, in our schools, and at work every time we compare our children, our students, or our employees to some vision of the perfect child, the perfect pupil, or the perfect teammate. To pursue this ideal of perfection means we consent that there is only one answer, only one proper way of being for the multitude of beings on this planet.

Is it possible for us to embrace a better, more nourishing, and more accepting worldview? One in which we each enter this world with hidden gifts? Talents that only we uniquely possess? Our mission in this alternate reality is to discover and nurture these gifts, slowly and methodically like the polishing of unformed stone into a tool, a dish, or a statue, each useful in its own right.

Our mission in this alternate reality, should we choose to live in it, is to see these gifts glimmering inside others and to help them discover and nurture their talents—to help them unveil what lies underneath their own unformed stone. This act of seeing deeply in others the glimmer of their hidden gifts, no matter how overwhelming their faults and limitations, is compassion.

I JOIN the crowd in a round of applause for Tanya. There she stood, up on the stage, holding a crushed can of Rockstar Energy Drink and with a smile on her face. She is the recipient of the Rockstar award at our quarterly all-team meeting. It wasn't that long ago when I sat down with Tanya in a conference room and explained to her how she wasn't meeting performance expectations on the team. As the applause for Tanya's achievements continued, I reflected on what changed.

Tanya won the Rockstar award for having delivered step-change improvement in our product's reliability, while at the same time reducing the amount of engineering effort we were spending on product upkeep. It was the ultimate holy grail: better results with less cost. Tanya had a penchant for numbers, loved working with engineers, and was masterful at finding simple answers to complex problems. She had explained to me how she loved the thrill of solving puzzles: the harder the puzzle, the more thrilling the pursuit.

Rewind the clock a year, and you find me sitting down with an entirely different Tanya.

"I am worried that you're not moving fast enough to come up

with a customer service plan for this upcoming launch," I explained. "And when you propose plans, they seem half-baked."

Tanya nods in quiet acceptance and says nothing. Over the next few months she continued to appear disinterested and slow to move with her work. Eventually the day of the launch of this new product came and went. Having completed her role in the project, it was time for Tanya to transition to her next assignment. We had a couple of options for what she could work on next. I discussed these options with her and she chose the project that would later earn her the Rockstar award.

I didn't know it at that time, but Tanya has ADHD and the customer service project bored her out of her mind. It leaned too heavily towards project management and was very operational in nature, with almost no engagement with engineering. It required the type of attention to detail where the prize goes to those who can dot the most I's and cross the most T's, not the type of attention to detail that rewards those who can find the one hidden key that unlocks the whole puzzle. The customer service project demanded strengths in all the areas where Tanya was weak. Little did I know how much of a difference a change in her role could make. I don't always have the ability to provide employees with options for what they work on, and it's not always the case that a good fit exists between our employees, their strengths, and the roles available on the team. I was glad the stars aligned for Tanya that day. We may not have uncovered her hidden talent otherwise.

It was five o'clock on a Thursday afternoon. I'm on a bus, crossing Lake Washington on the 520 bridge from Seattle to Bellevue. I'm making my way home from a long day at work. I recognize someone seated across from me.

It's Amanda.

She smiles and says hello. It's been several years since I last saw her. After a brief discussion about the current state of traffic she thanks me.

"I was failing there," she says. "I was trying to be who I was not. I'm now at another company. I am happy, and I am thriving."

We promise to stay connected and I find her on LinkedIn.

Several years later she appears on my LinkedIn feed with a new role notification. She's just been promoted to a director level position at a large software service company.

I smile.

Wainwright Yu

WAINWRIGHT YU is a technology executive and as a leadership coach who supports neurodivergent individuals as they discover and harness their (often hidden) strengths. He studied philosophy and accounting, an unusual combination that turned out to be a perfect fit for his neurodivergent brain, and has an MBA from Stanford. He is married to Jaine, his loving wife of over fifteen years. They have four multi-exceptional children.

NINETEEN

The Dates That Shape Us

Aaron Fromm

I sn't it weird how certain dates stand out in your life? And how what happens on those dates can quickly cause you to change course? Don't worry, this isn't going to be a sad story. Although it will start with a gut punch, it will show how important it is to have people you can count on to help guide and at times prop you up when the going gets tough.

I've always been one to assign meaning to certain dates and even more so to anniversaries. If you mention September 11 to anyone there is a shared sense of loss and anger, myself included. But I also choose to remember that date as my parents' wedding anniversary and all the happy memories that I had growing up. I still feel the shared loss that we had as a nation on that day, but I've always been someone that needs to live with the hope that given the right support, good things will happen. Even almost a quarter-century after the events of that day, I call my mother to wish her a happy anniversary.

You probably noticed that I didn't say I called to wish my mother and father a happy anniversary. The reason is I can't. He passed away too young from cancer on October 9, 2008. It's a date that will forever be seared in my memory.

I've come to learn that I was lucky. My father was present and was there to teach and guide me as I grew up. In the years since his passing I've learned of how many other people he helped. He was always there to listen, to help you think through a problem, or to help you find a solution. Friends still share stories of how my father helped them through a rough spot and, by doing so, changed the trajectory of their lives.

He always led from a spot of love and compassion.

When his friends learned that he was sick, they dropped everything and rushed to his bed. Six months after his passing, at a memorial to celebrate his life, he had friends, relatives, and coworkers all show up to raise a glass, eat way too much food, and share stories about how Jeffery Fromm had been there to guide them through some aspect of their career or life. To this day I still have people come up to me and say the words, "You're Jeff Fromm's son." It's been sixteen years since his passing.

Looking back on it, I never realized how much compassion my father really had. I knew he was always there for his family, but he was also there for a lot of other people, helping to lead them through some of the hardest moments in their lives and careers.

Going back to that day, October 9, I vividly remember sharing with my father that my wife and I were looking to start our family. I don't know if he heard me, but little did I know that October 9 would be the beginning of a much longer journey than expected.

Fast forward a couple of years and my wife and I are sitting in a doctor's office. We hear the dreaded words that as a couple you're never prepared to hear. *You will not be able to have children of your own.* Gut punch. In that moment I felt like I was in a Guy Ritchie film, with the camera stabilized on my stunned face and the rest of the world moving around me in a chaotic fashion. The thought running through my head was that I had failed as a husband and that our family name ended with me. It was a horrible thing to think, but that's where your mind goes.

The only thing I remember from the ride home is how quiet it was. It took a while for my wife and I to find the words. When we did, we cried and tried to make sense of what had just happened. To be honest, you really can't. There's no one to blame and no one to complain to.

Unconsciously I started to tap into some of the lessons that my father had taught me about compassion. I remembered something that he told me about taking perspective on a problem. It's important to mention that he was an attorney. He would ask if someone was dead or in jail. If you answered no to both questions then it wasn't that bad—you just had to think creatively and come up with a new solution. This didn't make us feel any better, but the thought was coming from a place of caring and compassion. It made me smile and allowed my wife and I to get creative on how to start our family.

Our first thought was to adopt. At the time international adoptions were the only thing we knew about and seemed way too complex. We knew that there were children in the United States who needed families and pairing that with the fact that my wife and I were in our late thirties and early forties we went down the path of fostering to adopt. And, man, were we in for a lesson in humility.

As we started the process of getting certified for foster care, we found out that where we lived the local agencies preferred to reunite children with biological kin. Case in point: when we were going through our certification class, one set of foster parents introduced themselves as the great-great-grandparents of two children of whom they were taking emergency placement. For those of you that don't know what the heck I'm talking about, this means that the local county agency had to go back two generations before they could find a family member willing to take responsibility for two children, both under the age of five. I was both floored by this couple's compassion and terrified for them and what they were wanting to take on. But my wife and I should have seen this as an omen of what we were about to run into.

We went through the class portion of the certification process, and as part of the home study portion the state requires both foster parents to go through an exhaustive background check. And when I say exhaustive, I mean grab you by the ankles and shake you upside down to see what falls out. They look at your finances, your employment, what you do for fun—is your yard fenced, if you have covers over the window wells in your basement, if you ever been accused of a crime (accused, not convicted)—do you have any traffic tickets, do you have a baby crib in the house (the only piece of furniture we needed to have), and whether it's your end goal to adopt.

It was the last one that got us. We did want to adopt and have a family, and as the state's objective was to reunite children with kin, we were advised to seek private adoption. It could have taken years for foster-to-adopt to happen, so we dropped out of the foster care system and looked into private adoption.

Back to the drawing board, we applied my father's two-word criteria—was anyone dead or in prison? Nope. We took a bit of time, looked into foreign adoption, and by this time there were either political issues holding up adoptions or our ages meant we had "aged out" for some countries. Not wanting to have to be denied again, we decided against international adoption. But we did find another option.

My accountant, who also knew my father, introduced us to a local adoption agency. We loved this team—they were working with local families and doing really good work. We started our journey with them in October of 2017. It wasn't October 9, but it was close enough. We flew through all our background checks, we knew what to expect from the foster process, and we flew through our home study—heck, we even had a crib ready to go.

Five years went by and it was approaching the fourteenth anniversary of my father's death. Most years I make the trek up to the mountains where we scattered my father's ashes, but this year I wasn't really feeling it. We had just completed our most recent home study to keep current for the adoption process and there's a form that you fill out that is simply headed, "When it's time to stop." It's an important document, and its purpose is to allow my wife and I to put into words when it's been too long and it's time to move on with our lives. The goal is, you fill out this document when you're not emotional or tired and refer to it when you need to make a tough decision.

My wife and I decided to give it another year. We didn't have high hopes, we had a few close calls, but nothing really panned out.

Then it happened.

If you've ever had one of those moments where you will never forget where you were—mine was next to the butter and cream cheese at my local supermarket. Well, kind of. I didn't pick up the phone, I let the unknown caller ID go to voice mail and continued picking out butter. Next thing I knew my wife texted me three words: "CALL ME NOW."

Apparently, she said yes even before I got home. Our state has open adoptions, which means the birth mother and birth father get to pick who the child will be placed with. This normally happens in the third trimester, and you have three to four months to get everything in order. We had fifteen minutes. This is referred to as a stork drop. Surprise, no time to think, no time to call anyone—and no time to buy any of the necessities. Did I mention our crib didn't have a mattress? Luckily our neighbors' youngest had just outgrown his infant seat. They were out putting up Halloween decorations and we told them the news and asked if we could borrow the car seat. No problem, it's in the garage and they'll drop it off later. "We kind of need it *now*."

We get to the hospital and meet the most beautiful baby boy that I have ever seen. Our case worker tell us he hasn't been named yet.

Did I mention it was October 9?

It was the day my father passed fourteen years earlier, and the day that my son was born, *and* his grandfather had been born exactly 74 years earlier. Yes, my father died on his sixtieth birthday. He would have thought that was really funny. There was only one name that the baby boy could have, Jeffery.

Leading with compassion doesn't mean you'll be spared from making difficult decisions. It's about making sure that compassion is our starting point. Compassion needs to take the lead position in any decision-making process. The life my father lived guides the path I choose today for myself, and for my family. This gift of compassion has changed my own life's trajectory.

Having love and compassion, and making sure no one died or is in jail along the way, has gotten me to where I am today. I hope to share the same wisdom with Jeff.

Aaron Fromm

Aaron Fromm is the founder of AZF Business Strategy and Consulting, helping organizations leverage the power of intelligent automation and artificial intelligence. He has over twenty-five years of experience as a software engineer and technical consulting leader, helping organizations leverage complex technologies to transform the way they do business. Aaron believes that when used correctly technology can give us back the one asset we will never get more of: Time.

TWENTY

Compassion in Action: Where Does it Begin?

Jaspal Bajwa

The third-century BCE Mauryan emperor Ashoka was known to be a cruel and ruthless warrior.

Through a string of conquests he expanded the boundaries of his empire until it reached an unrivaled status. After emerging victorious from a particularly difficult battle at Kalinga, he sat pensively on a rock. The battlefield was strewn with thousands of corpses.

Deeply troubled by the devastation that lay before him, he noticed a few Buddhist monks passing by. Hearing the laments of the seriously wounded, the monks had stopped to tend to them. Their faces radiated equanimity and, watching this act of compassion, something inside Ashoka changed.

When he arose he was a transformed man.

The king began to advocate following the Buddhist philosophy, especially the values of *karuna* (compassion) and *metta* (love). He went on to institute the code of *dharma*, the principles of rightful conduct in life. He encouraged the energetic practice of virtues like honesty, truthfulness, compassion, mercifulness, benevolence, nonviolence, moderation, and considerate behavior toward all beings. Emissaries, including his own children, were sent to neighboring countries—as far afield as South Eastern Asia and China—to spread his message. In time his reign became known for its progressiveness, thanks to compassionate leadership.

Not surprisingly, history remembers him as Ashoka the Great.

An early lesson about compassion

My own transformative change happened much more quickly.

While still at business school, during a soccer match an overhead scissor kick went terribly wrong. On landing, I shattered my ankle and passed out. As I was wheeled out of surgery, I looked at the heavy cast-ridden leg and the crutches with dismay. The foreboding of losing an academic year loomed large.

Back at the hostel, seven classmates spontaneously came together to help me. Every single day, their acts of innovative and compassionate care ensured I did not miss any class activity. The unconditional support I received gave me a renewed understanding of humility, gratitude and compassion. This was further underlined for me as I became aware of my own frailty. Till then I had nursed the notion of being a sort of super-human. I thought I could climb any mountain.

This accident taught me it was okay not to be a perfectionist. Instead, it was more important to develop robust self-esteem, to nurture a sense of self-worth and invest in building required competencies.

This lesson in compassion in action stayed on with me in my later years. With each rough and tumble of life, I started reflecting on the downs in the roller-coaster of life. The potential these held for transformation fascinated me. I was able to tap into a sense of finding meaning and having an abundance of joy, helping me recognize and respect the diversity each team member brought to the table.

Regardless of organizational size or its cultural context, over the course of my career one thing became increasingly clear to me: inspirational leadership always starts at the top.

Learn, unlearn, re-learn

In my career in the consumer goods industry, I quickly took on the practice of regularly visiting the marketplace and the manufacturing shop floor because I knew that that was where the action would be. That was where I'd learn the most. Before arriving at a site, I would make it a point to study the local context and show respect for the lived experiences of the team and the specific culture of the organization. I discovered that reciprocity, namely understanding that everyone is a leader in their own domain, could help lay the foundation for mutual respect and trust. In times of challenge and crisis, this ensured we appreciated each other's vantage points. Regardless of differences, we were always able to reach across the table to arrive at the best solution under the circumstances.

If I were to take a step back and review the three decades in which I was fortunate to have served in both strategic staff roles as well as profit-center head roles across multiple continents, I can recall at least three clear instances of how I continued to learn, unlearn and re-learn about what it takes to be a 'whole' human being both at the level of the individual self, as well as for the collective (as a family or team or community).

Almost always, I've learned, each of our development journeys starts with ourselves.

I learned to give permission to **accept** myself. Equally, the grace to **accept** situational ground reality. I made it a practice to be mindfully **aware** of the conscious choices, I had the option to exercise. Importantly, how an alternate **reframing** lens would help me transform my perspective, thus helping me co-create literally a 'new world' for myself. Over time, I evolved a more compassionate life mantra: *learn, unlearn, re-learn … so as to serve.*

Once I began this process of healing and becoming whole once again, I invariably found myself much better positioned to practice compassion and to be of service to a shared cause far larger than myself.

Three episodes from my corporate life stand out.

1. **Treating each being with dignity.** In some corporate cultures, command and control is the system *de rigueur,* and yet we are not simply employees, we are human beings. I made it a point to treat each employee with utmost respect. In one of my assignments, I was heading a major turnaround. Nearly ten thousand employees of a leading pharmaceutical company were engaged in serving patient needs across a major chunk of the globe, and stress was rife. Therefore, we set up a country-specific, single-window helpdesk. Ensuring psychological safety—a key requirement for building trust—unleashed huge amounts of positive relational energy. Everyone was more considerate of the conditions the other functional teams were working under. As we fostered an organization-wide winning culture, a snowball-like momentum fueled a positive upward spiral.

2. **Walking in someone else's shoes**. Working in silos is different from building and nurturing cross-functional alignment, collaboration and team spirit, the latter being a much sought-after goal for every CEO. And it is not always easy. A Me/Mine syndrome often prevails. For me, since my early career was in new product development and marketing this lesson came easy. I realized very early that if I could not invite and include all key players who could support my project, the chances of success would get dramatically affected. So, I made it a point to let off my ego-ridden pride ('my project', 'my functional area', etc.) and always reach out to a wide and diverse group, across the aisle. I used every skill I possessed to make them feel I was there to actively listen and seek feed-forward in an open and non-judgemental manner. The key in this was to make each constituency feel genuinely respected for what they stood for and what they brought to the table.

3. **Coming together and walking away with compassion.** During my professional tenure, letting go

of employees for reasons of integrity was not difficult. Yet, each time it had to be done with compassion. There are times when we have to call out persistent lack of performance but rather than being quick on the trigger to hire and fire at will, I always advocated a more compassionate approach. Colleagues and teammates were asked to chip in to help raise the lagging manager's performance. But if the long rope still did not yield the desired results, we let the concerned manager know that continuing to remain on board was a disservice to the rest of the team. This compassionate way of letting go helped them move to an environment that better suited their skills.

The seven As

A beautiful legend comes to mind that underlines the fact that compassion always starts with the self.

In the Himalayas, about 2500 years ago, the young prince Siddhartha was kept sheltered inside castle walls. One day when he emerged and witnessed the suffering all around him, he was deeply moved. This led him to ask a key question: *Why suffering?* After years of practicing deep inquiry, he finally arose from under the Bodhi tree (the tree of meditation) to become known as the Buddha. The beauty of being born as a human is that each one of us can choose to reflect on the choices we make. Discovering our own humanity is a journey.

Being together in the trenches, sharing the camaraderie of blood, sweat, and tears makes us forget our differences. We learn to let go of previous biases and rigidities and focus instead on our shared humanity.

Compassion is a deep and multi-textured human value. And it is entirely possible to be inspired to explore it and embed it into our day-to-day life. One way is to deeply observe everything inside ourselves and our environment. Make the most of experiential learning.

As we go through life's experiences, we can always choose to self-coach ourselves using this 'A's framework:

1. **Ask.** Have the humility to ask, with courage, curiosity and compassion. Venture out.
2. **Awareness and Acceptance of the reality as it is.** Allow it to ripple out towards quantum infinity.
3. **Align** with the shared purpose or cause you have chosen to commit to.
4. **Accept.** Adapt with grace to an ever-changing world affected by volatility, uncertainty, complexity and ambiguity (VUCA).
5. **Authenticity-in-Action.** Achieve flow. Aim for resonance with your internal moral compass/values *and* invest in relationships with the so-called "Other'. Modify recurrent behaviors to down-regulate negative emotions *and* upregulate positive emotional attractors which release endorphins and leverage the parasympathetic nervous system opening us to invite change and growth in our lives.
6. **Alchemy.** Never underestimate the power of transformational change. For self. As well as for the 'other'. Discovering our own humanity is a journey. This journey is best traveled in company. Alchemy can happen in a flash (as in '*satori*'), or it can take a lifetime of experiential learning. Either way it is Wow!
7. **Appreciate the wholeness of each being and the fullness of life.** Enjoy the journey.

Jaspal Bajwa

As an executive coach and a team coach, **JASPAL BAJWA** partners to ignite excellence. His Success by Design consulting practice, Sunya Circle, is informed by three decades in operational roles in global corporations. Co-creating significant and sustainable value through organizational vitality is his continuing passion as he coaches business leaders and their teams to thrive with an enduring sense of joy.

TWENTY-ONE

All Behavior is an Expression of an Unmet Need

Scott Gauvin

I was stretched thin constantly traveling for work, managing early parenthood, building a new business, and dedicating time to a non-profit. Every day felt like a balancing act with too much to do and never enough time. I accepted that overextension was my normal. When asked to evaluate a program for the non-profit I supported I hesitated—I didn't have the time, energy, or emotional bandwidth. Yet despite my reluctance, I agreed. I was fulfilling my responsibilities out of duty, but I felt restless with my decision.

On the second day of the three-day evaluation session, I sat in a brightly lit training room with large windows overlooking an atrium. My mind drifted between my to-do list and the plants growing high on the walls. I wondered how they managed to water them. The conversation in the room covered familiar territory—communication skills in the workplace—until one phrase pulled me sharply back into focus: "All behavior is an expression of an unmet need."

The instructor said it so plainly, as if it were common knowledge. My instinct was to reject it. No way, I thought, that let's everyone off the hook for their behavior. I started playing out scenarios in my head and looking for exceptions. But every scenario

I ran through either confirmed it or led me to a harsh judgement about the other person's behavior. I began applying it to moments in my own life, years of actions and behaviors—especially the ones I wasn't proud of. Patterns I hadn't fully understood started to emerge. No, I thought again, it's too simple. But the more I explored, the clearer it became. There was always an unmet need driving my behavior.

I was overwhelmed with mixed emotions. I felt excitement at the clarity this brought, but frustration and anger for not realizing it sooner. Then guilt, as I thought about how my unmet needs had affected the people I cared about. This simple phrase connected dots I'd struggled with for years. My difficulty in connecting and trusting others was rooted in needs I hadn't even acknowledged.

The weight of unspoken emotions and unmet needs had quietly taken control of my life without realizing it. By ignoring my own struggles, I had shaped the way I interacted with the world around me. For the first time I could see how my frustration, defensiveness, and disconnection all traced back to my own unexpressed needs. The simple phrase unlocked something deep within me and prompted me to question: Why did I react the way I did? What was the need?

GROWING UP, my relationships with others were often fraught with tension. This was most obvious with my mother. She was a single teenage mother raising two kids in the projects, doing everything she could to provide. We survived on public assistance, and though I didn't recognize it when I was younger we were caught in a system that labeled us as "lazy." I had a visceral reaction to any insinuation that I was lazy. I didn't realize how deeply those societal judgments had embedded themselves in my psyche until I started to reflect on it.

In retrospect I can see how I attempted to combat those stereotypes, even at an early age. At eight years old I was already determined to prove I wasn't lazy. I would walk across the street, help strangers load their groceries for a quarter, or sell roses I cut from the bushes near our building. These entrepreneurial efforts were praised and gave me a sense of purpose, but looking back I realize they were also a way to escape the instability I felt at home. My drive to prove I wasn't lazy was a way to assert control in an environment where I often felt powerless.

Behind that ambition lay the more complicated reality of my relationship with my mother. Our home was filled with emotional distance, drinking, and a revolving door of boyfriends. I had learned early on to keep my relationships superficial, avoiding vulnerability as a means of self-protection. My business ventures were, in a way, my distraction—a way to focus on something I could control while avoiding the painful emotions stirring beneath the surface. Getting close to people was difficult and if someone did try to breakthrough I'd usually find a way to sabotage it.

The real wound—the one I had avoided confronting for years—was deeply rooted in my relationship with my mother. I spent so much of my life wanting her love, approval, and attention, but constantly frustrated by her emotional absence. I didn't understand why she couldn't give me what I needed, and that left me feeling abandoned, even when she was physically present. Growing up in a home filled with uncertainty only reinforced that feeling of abandonment. But what I had failed to recognize then, and what took me years to truly grasp, was that she was fighting with her own demons.

Looking back now, I can see that my mother was doing the best she could with the limited tools she had. She was struggling too—emotionally, financially, and personally—but at the time all I could focus on was what I wasn't getting from her. I didn't realize how much her behavior was driven by her own fears, her unhealed wounds, and her unmet needs. As I reflected on this idea of unmet needs, it helped me start unraveling my own pain. I began to see how much of my behavior was driven by the unmet needs I had buried deep inside.

I came to understand that our conflict wasn't just about our differences. It was about a profound misunderstanding of each other's unmet needs. For years I had viewed her actions through the lens of my own pain and frustration. Now for the first time, I was able to see her as more than just my mother who had somehow come up short of my own needs. I saw her as a person who had struggled, sacrificed, and done her best in a world that had never made it easy for her.

This realization didn't just change how I saw her—it changed me. I stopped expecting her to be the person I had always wanted her to be and started trying to understand her for who she was. I let go of the blame, the anger, and the disappointment. Instead, I began approaching our interactions with more empathy, listening more carefully, and letting go of my need to be right or to point out how she was wrong. The walls between us didn't come down overnight but each conversation felt a little less tense, a little more honest. For the first time, I wasn't just speaking to my mother—I was beginning to truly hear and see her.

Now, faced with being a parent myself, I couldn't help but reflect on how I might be coming up short of my own children's needs. How were my own needs getting in the way of their needs? How were my needs getting in the way of my wife, my friends, and my clients. This exploration in my mind began to explode. Reflecting back on old conversations, judgements, arguments, lost relationships. I realized that my reactions, like others', were driven by fears and unmet needs. My defensiveness, mistrust, and quickness to anger were all rooted in a deep fear of abandonment and a need to feel seen and valued. Once I understood that about myself, I could start to extend that understanding to others. I was suddenly motivated to do something.

This new knowledge gave me a new desire to revisit some of those conversations. As I started to listen to others, I could more easily see the unmet needs that drove the behaviors, the decisions, the reactions. I was starting to see the humanity in others in a way that wasn't previously obvious to me. I could see their fears, their wounds, their hopes—and was recognizing that their behavior, like mine, came from a place of unmet needs.

. . .

It took years for me to fully understand what I had uncovered. It was compassion. Compassion isn't just kindness—it's recognizing someone's humanity, accepting their flaws, and supporting them without judgment. This was harder than I expected, especially after a lifetime of feeling judged myself. It required humility to face my own shortcomings and courage to begin repairing the relationships that mattered most.

Repairing my relationship with my mother wasn't easy, and I will admit it's still a work in progress. For years I was quick to argue and often shut down when old wounds were triggered. But as I began to approach her with compassion—listening without judgment and trying to truly understand her pain—everything started to shift. I no longer saw her as the source of my frustration but as someone with her own story.

Slowly our conversations became more open and honest, even when we discussed difficult topics. For the first time, I wasn't afraid of rejection, and that allowed me to be generous—with my patience, my understanding, and my forgiveness. I let go of the need to always be right or to get validation from her, and this created more space for kindness and connection.

This transformation didn't just affect my relationship with my mother; it rippled into all of my relationships. In my marriage, compassion helped me navigate the stresses of parenting and running a business without turning stress into conflict. By being more generous with my mother—offering understanding and patience without expecting anything in return—I could extend that same generosity to my wife. I no longer approached challenges in our relationship seeking something in return. Instead I gave support and empathy freely, creating a more open space for both of us. In my friendships I became more present, less reactive, and more willing to listen.

In my professional life, I began to see how leading with compassion transformed relationships. What had once felt purely transactional now became opportunities for genuine connection. I couldn't help but think of my grandmother, a factory worker who endured long, grueling days just to get by.

Years later, as I worked alongside people facing similar challenges, I saw the same struggles she had—overlooked and undervalued while striving to make ends meet. This shaped how I approached leadership, reminding me that behind every push for improvement are real people, often judged unfairly and labeled as lazy. Recognizing their unmet needs helped me lead with compassion, rather than focusing solely on cost savings, productivity, and efficiency.

Leadership, I came to understand, wasn't just about driving results. True leadership meant creating an environment where people felt valued, seen, heard, and understood. While improving a production line, I met Catherine, an employee on the verge of quitting due to conflicts with a disrespectful co-worker. Seeing her potential, I suggested moving her to another line but a mix-up the next day placed her back with the same co-worker. She walked out and quit. Management dismissed the situation and blamed her for leaving. I suggested reaching out, and they agreed to give her another chance if I called her. When I did, Catherine explained she couldn't return because she didn't have a ride, so I offered to pick her up and help her find her place in the company. Over time she thrived and eventually became one of their top employees.

Leading with compassion meant looking past Catherine's frustration to understand what she needed to succeed. It wasn't about lowering expectations or avoiding accountability—it was about helping people overcome obstacles, fostering open and respectful conversations, and offering support instead of giving up on them.

Looking back, compassion didn't just heal my relationship with my family and friends—it transformed how I connected with those around me. It deepened my relationships, gave my work new purpose, and helped me show up in the world with greater authenticity and empathy. Leading with compassion is not a single act; it's a daily practice. It requires checking in with ourselves, recognizing our own wounds and triggers, and choosing to care instead of judging, even when it's inconvenient. But in doing so we create the conditions for true connection and meaningful change—from the inside out.

That reluctant decision to attend the training session became the start of something far greater than I could ever have imagined. Leading with compassion, I learned, is not a weakness. It is a powerful force that can heal, transform, and create a better world—one relationship at a time. One behavior at a time. One unmet need at a time.

Scott Gauvin

Scott Gauvin is a management consultant and Lean specialist with thirty years of experience helping organizations transform the way they perceive and pursue performance. As CEO of Macresco and co-founder of the Respect for People Roadmap, he's partnered with organizations worldwide and across industries to innovate their business and operating models and put people at the center of their corporate and operations strategies.

The Strength in Conscious Awareness

Compassion is fueled by understanding and accepting that we're all made of strength and struggle. Compassion is not a practice of "better than" or "I can fix you"—it's a practice based in the beauty and pain of shared humanity.[1]

Brené Brown

TWENTY-TWO

Trans(forming) the Weight of My Own Expectations

Sabrina Riley

M y mom always wanted the best for me. Growing up in a home with conservative, traditional values, her vision of "the best" meant excelling in school. From a young age, maybe as early as third grade, she knew I was very capable of great things.

"You can do anything you put your mind to," she would often remind me.

I remember one afternoon vividly. I came home with a C as a mid-term grade on my report card. I could see the disappointment in her eyes and feel it in her voice. She knew I could do better, that I wasn't living up to my potential.

I felt the weight of needing to please her, the unspoken demand to do better, to prove that I was worthy of her love. Although her disappointment stung, I never thought much of it because it worked at the time. I improved and I can count on one hand the classes in which I received less than a B.

My mom's tough love felt like the key to success. As a teenager I started associating her love with my achievements in school and sports, believing that love was conditional and based on how well I did. Even though I logically understood her love, I often misunderstood her actions and intentions. I constantly sought her approval but I was missing something I didn't even know how to ask for—a sense of being loved unconditionally.

The only sport I excelled at growing up was bowling. From my first coach at ten years old to my teammates in high school, everyone told me I was gifted. I had learned to perform under pressure and developed high expectations for myself. At one point in high school, I was on multiple teams, practicing or competing four to five times a week. But if I didn't live up to my own standards, I couldn't accept it. I was relentless in my pursuit of perfection, driven by that same belief that my worth was tied to my performance.

I can still vividly remember the state championship game. I was seventeen years old, standing with my high school team—supposedly on top of the world. We were considered a dream team, but as I stood there I felt like an outsider in my own body. We were winning easily, yet the lack of my own worth was growing stronger.

I couldn't put my finger on it then, but something was deeply wrong. It was as if the joy that should have come with the victory was just out of reach. All I could feel was numbness. I remember looking at my teammates, celebrating and laughing, but I felt detached. It was like watching a movie where I was present but not truly participating. I had built so much of my identity around being a top performer, and yet at this pinnacle moment I felt more lost than ever. The victory didn't fulfill me. Instead it left me feeling empty and unworthy—as if I hadn't earned the success we achieved.

That day I began to sense the disconnect between external achievements and self-compassion. It felt like two parallel tracks—one labeled "success" and the other labeled "contentment"—that never intersected. No matter how far or fast I ran on the track of achievement, contentment and joy seemed out of reach. There was an ache inside of me that whispered, *This can't be all that there is.* It wasn't just the emptiness I felt standing there at the top, it was the growing awareness that each victory was slipping through my fingers. I kept thinking, *If winning feels this hollow what's the point?* But I didn't have the language to articulate that feeling. So I did what I had always done and I toughened up, pushed harder, and performed even better. I was clinging to the hope that if I could somehow meet the ever-looming expectations, maybe then I'd feel worthy of love, success, and joy. But that day at the state championship was the first crack in that belief. It marked the slow unraveling of the mindset that for so long had been the foundation of my identity.

Fast forward to my relationship with my ex-wife. She and I spent most of the last four out of five years together. One of my biggest regrets is how hard I was on her. She often told me that I was too critical and my harshness left her feeling unloved. This was especially true when it came to her career. Over the course of our relationship she had a handful of jobs, none of which brought her fulfillment. She battled mental health challenges, including some severe anxiety, and some of the jobs were so draining that she would come home completely depleted.

I'll never forget the toll her job as a recruiter took on her. She despised it and it was sucking the life out of her. Yet we weren't in a good place financially and I had already spent almost a decade worrying about money. I was working as hard as I could to make more commission at my job and take pressure off her. It never felt like enough.

I hoped that if she worked as hard as she could we could be happier. We could lift that financial pressure and enjoy more experiences such as going out to dinner, taking more vacations, and just enjoying life together. I thought if she could succeed at her job, she would finally see her own worth and love herself more.

But instead my lack of compassion sunk her deeper into self-loathing and sadness. She began to feel like I would only love her if she were successful. She never told me outright, but I know in my heart that my version of tough love was a major reason why she left. Even after she left it took me almost another year to understand what compassion truly meant.

It's almost comical to me how hard I have been on myself in the last year. I've only recently discovered myself as a transgender woman, and yet I expected myself to have it all figured out. I expected to be thriving in every aspect of my life. It's insane really. Most of my life has been filled with misery and I am just beginning to understand what it means to love myself and build a life that feels authentic. I am still learning what it means to interact with the world as my true self.

And yet I've burned myself out. Again.

It's a cycle I've repeated more times than I can count.

I'll experience a few months of success, especially in my career. This is followed by long stretches of frustration, disappointment, and self-criticism. I try new strategies, push myself harder, but nothing seems to work. I can't help but think back to my childhood when school came easily to me. Why has my career been so much harder? Am I not as capable as my mom once believed?

The answer lay in learning compassion, both for myself and for others.

At first, compassion felt almost impossible to practice. I spent so long punishing myself for not living up to the rigid standards I had internalized from society and from my upbringing. Turning to compassion felt like admitting weakness, like I was letting myself off the hook for not being perfect. But embracing compassion wasn't really a choice. It became inevitable because nothing else worked. The constant pressure to perform, to measure up, and to strive for external validation kept burning me out.

For years I had lived under the weight of these standards, but as a transgender woman redefining my life, I found myself questioning everything.

I was questioning society's norms, everyone's ideas of success, and even what it meant to lead with compassion. Every expectation I had clung to suddenly felt like it belonged to someone else, like a suit I had worn my whole life that was never tailored for me. I realized none of what I had learned thus far was made with someone like me in mind. Success, as I had been taught, was about fitting into a system that wasn't built to accommodate my truth. It felt as though I had been chasing a dream that would never belong to me, trying to thrive in a structure that didn't see or value who I really was.

There was a profound sense of truth in discovering myself as a transgender woman—a truth that felt as undeniable as the air I breathed. That same clarity began to ripple in other areas of my life. If this truth about my identity could be so powerful, what other beliefs had I been carrying that needed to be dismantled? Compassion, I realized, had to start with me. Not as a reward for meeting someone else's definition of success, but as a practice of honoring who I am at every stage of my journey. Society's version of success demanded relentless effort and sacrifice, but compassion invited me to rest, to pause, and to say, "I am enough right here, right now."

Finding compassion didn't happen overnight. It was a slow process of unlearning the narratives I had internalized for so long.

The first step was simply noticing. Noticing how harsh I was with myself. By consciously observing the way I spoke to myself, I could see clearly how it made me feel. I could feel the need to prove myself so clearly. That inner child just wanted to be seen. But she had no idea she needed to be seen for who she truly is—not for what she is capable of accomplishing. The voice of my inner critic was so loud that I hadn't even realized how much it was dictating my life. It felt like I was constantly punishing myself for not being good enough.

As I started noticing the inner critic and the lack of compassion, I started questioning it out loud. I asked myself, "What if I treated myself the way I would treat someone else I care about?"

The answer struck me like a bolt of lightning. Of course I couldn't find compassion for myself because I was taught tough love from such a young age. I didn't understand what it meant to truly love yourself unconditionally. All I knew was that love involved pushing yourself and others to "be the best." I had to learn that compassion wasn't about letting myself off the hook for mistakes, but about creating space to be human. Instead of tearing myself down for every failure, I began to practice acknowledging my efforts and my humanity. This didn't change overnight. I had to constantly remind myself that I didn't need to be perfect to be deserving of my love or anyone else's. I had to constantly remind myself that I am undoing twenty-nine years of a damaging inner critic.

Redefining compassion as a transgender woman wasn't just about how I treated myself. It also meant shifting how I view success and leadership. Society teaches us that you climb the ladder by sacrificing yourself in the name of achievement. You push as hard as you possibly can at all costs because that climbing is where you will find fulfillment.

By learning to have compassion for myself I've been able to redefine success on my own terms. Success to me is caring for myself so I can live out my purpose and impact the world. Success is no longer pushing myself to the brink of exhaustion for someone else's dream. I can allow myself to be proud of who I am, not just for what I have accomplished.

I'll be honest, I am still working on compassion. I've come a long way in the last year and yet I still have so far to go. There are days I fall back into my old patterns, days where my inner critic takes the reins. Those days I forget how to be kind to myself. But I'm learning to have compassion for those moments too.

I'm learning that there is power in just noticing these moments and allowing myself to get back on track.

I'm learning that growth doesn't have to be perfect, that progress isn't linear, and that I am worthy of love and compassion at every stage of the journey. Not just when I'm at my best, but when I'm struggling too.

Sabrina Riley

Sabrina Riley is a transformational leadership consultant, writer, and speaker passionate about authenticity and personal growth. With over fifteen years of expertise, she empowers individuals to embrace self-compassion and self-awareness as essential tools for navigating life's challenges. As a transgender woman, Sabrina brings unique insight into the journey of becoming one's truest self and through her consulting and storytelling she inspires others to create sustainable, aligned success grounded in authenticity.

TWENTY-THREE

What Would Rossi Do?

Blair Morris

"What would Rossi do?"

I flinched and cringed. I could feel the eyes of all my colleagues on me, waiting for my response.

"I'll do it with you if you do it!" he said.

And suddenly my colleague and I were on the floor, on our backs, in front of twenty-three people—wriggling back and forth with our legs and hands in the air just like my dog Rossi does when he is full of life and joy. The retreat room was full of laughter. It wasn't the laughter of derision but a joyous sound. It was the laughter of adults reveling in the freedom of being in the moment! I found myself laughing too, and filled with that joy and freedom. And I was not alone on that floor.

My life has been governed by two mostly unrecognized yet powerful beliefs. The first is that anything short of perfect is failure and the second that I am essentially alone. I never used to think of myself as a perfectionist and would frequently find myself really annoyed by others who exhibited perfectionist tendencies. Yes, classic psychological projectionism. However, I was always deeply compelled to get it right and make sure I knew everything about any subject for which I was responsible.

. . .

A DEEP FEAR of failure and not being good enough has been with me since before I can remember. As the middle of three girls, all close in age and with a mother who didn't handle stress well at all, the sense of being alone and solely responsible has been with me from my earliest years. I preferred to be alone and away from chaos.

And there I was, in my later 50s, in the process of starting a new career as a professional coach and in a training retreat with other coaches, having a rough time of it.

Years of entrenched perfectionism and fear of failure were being triggered and I was getting very down on myself for not being the perfect coach in the practice sessions.

Intellectually I could identify what was happening, espouse the benefits of being observed and getting feedback, and recognize the ways I needed to improve. But my body was reacting in many of the same ways it did when I was a young girl. I would freeze during a session. I was not present for my practice client. My brain was feeling disconnected and I could not find the words to ask discerning questions.

And then, to my horror, the tears came.

In this retreat each coaching practice group consisted of three people and we were all struggling to one degree or another when it was our turn to coach. While I was able to send positive vibes to each of my partners as they coached, I found myself not even thinking to do the same for myself. It was a very long day.

The next morning of the retreat started as did all others. We did our somatic group practices then came into a circle to debrief the previous days' experiences and lessons. I was still struggling and had not slept well either. Then it was my turn to talk, and the tears were back. That is when one of my coaching partners asked me, "What would Rossi do?" Rossi is my beautiful Australian Shepherd dog. He has the thickest, most luxurious black and white coat with accents of tan that I have ever seen on an Aussie. Evidently my partner recalled me talking about how full of joy and fun Rossi is—a true clown of a dog who loves having an audience of people laugh at him. In a previous discussion group, I had shared that Rossi is a consistent source of laughter and had been helping me reconnect with the presence of joy in life.

What would Rossi do? That was easy to answer but so very difficult to share out loud. Fear was already welling up inside of me as I realized where this was going.

I took a deep breath. "Rossi would be on the floor, on his back, wriggling like crazy to make everyone laugh," I shared.

They all looked at me and I became aware that I was feeling a wave of loving encouragement rise from the group. I flinched and cringed. When my partner offered to do it with me, I stared at him in disbelief, yet all I saw was the most compassionate, supportive, and caring face smiling back at me.

I was not alone. I was being held in deep support by people with whom I had only worked for a few months, and I could feel it deep in my body. And there I was, on the floor in the middle of a circle of chairs, on my back with my partner, wriggling around as best I could. Our hands and feet were waving in the air and all our colleagues were supporting us, laughing and feeling joy. In that moment those two childhood beliefs began to unravel, and my heart opened to how deeply held beliefs keep so many of us from inhabiting our potential.

Don't get me wrong. I know that my personal patterns arose to help me handle things when I was a small child and to a large degree they helped me to be successful in my roles in healthcare over a forty-year career. These patterns of perfectionism and fear of failure also drove my leadership style. I was known for being the one to bring in when things needed to get done—be it running a committee to solve a difficult problem, reorganizing a program, or launching a new department in the hospital environment. My projects ran well, I had a great grasp of strategy, goals were almost always met, my employee engagement scores were always the best, and I made sure that those above me looked great to their peers and the board. I was a model leader. But I was not the best leader I could have been. Those same patterns also limited me. The fear and perfectionism repeatedly kept me from taking risks that could have been very developmental over the years. They also ensured that my priority was my job and not my own growth or a balance with my family and personal life. And my employees would have really benefitted so much more if I had been able to be more present with them, their ideas, and their struggles.

On the floor of the retreat room, I was experiencing leadership that was different from any I had ever known in my career. It wasn't about my partner's needs or agenda, and it was not based in fear. To have someone, as my coaching partner was, be so fully present, holding me in complete compassion and regard, filled me with a deep sense of grace. And this, in turn, allowed for me to be okay with being in the messy space of learning, growing, and developing competence. And I was not alone. My partner did not ask me to channel Rossi on my own. He was a fully embodied leader and encouraged me to join him on the floor in front of the rest of the group. He too was struggling with the journey to competence, and might have had his own fears about what it would be like to be Rossi. But he clearly put those aside and was with me and supporting me. In leading this way, he was also supporting himself and the others. All of us were experiencing the challenges around learning to be great coaches. After our time on the floor several of our cohort shared that they had been experiencing similar struggles with the growth curve and were now feeling much better too.

IMAGINE a world where we all explored, uncovered, and released our limiting beliefs! This is the work that we leaders must embrace to be our best selves. And imagine a world where leaders understand the need for that same journey in their team members. When I teach and coach leaders who want to be their best selves, it's the foundational conscious leadership skills that we focus on. These are also the foundational skills of being good humans. The compassion with which I was held by my coaching partner that day is one of those foundational ways of being.

Connecting with others in our leadership work can be very superficial. Think of a time you sat down in a meeting before it started and the person sitting next to you asked how your day was going but was clearly disconnected. Were they asking, as so many of us do, because we have been taught that that is the polite thing to do? Now contrast that with a time where someone asked you and was clearly very present, patiently listening, and wanting to understand your experience of your day. That is something many of us may struggle to recall. They are few and far between, both at work and at home.

Leadership is not for the faint of heart and to do it well I contend that one must have a truly open heart. A great leader recognizes what it means to be human in our world and understands that every single one of us is as perfectly imperfect as every other human. That recognition allows for us to be able to connect with and understand another person's experiences along the whole spectrum—from the most very difficult to the most joyous. From there springs the desire to "take action" to help the person. That may include literal action to help them, or it may mean the desire to support the person by holding them in their thoughts, sending positive energy their direction, or even a hug if appropriate.

Workplace cultures are set by the leaders and having leaders who are strong enough to bring their hearts into their work is presently uncommon. That needs to change. The leaders at the helm of the organization need to role-model being fully present, truly listening, recognizing the humanity in the other person, then helping them through a challenge or just holding space for them while they find their way. The leader needs to understand that others have patterns like perfectionism, fear of failure—and so many others that could be worked through if the setting was right. The person who experiences that kind of leadership will then role-model and become that leader for those on their team.

Innovation, creativity, belonging, engagement, and well-being are all areas that are struggling in most organizations. Cultures are very driven by the level of awareness, presence, and compassion in their leaders. The constant pressure for stock values, attention, ever-growing profit margins, and power have led to an epidemic of leaders who are achieving goals but not connected with their own inner landscape. This disconnection has resulted in the above issues and many more—most of which have a deep negative impact. It is rare to find organizations that don't have cultures based in fear— fear of not making the budget or forecasts, fear of being acquired, fear of employee unionization, and so many more. Then there is the constant reliance on technical or quick-fix attempts instead of an effective approach to understanding the deeper and more insidious roots of issues. An unfortunately common example that I see repeated is offering employees access to free mental health counseling but not doing the harder work—the work of changing the paradigm to one where employees are supported and empowered to be part of solutions, instead of compelled to just work harder. And leaders wonder why the burnout and turnover continue.

We know that organizations of all types are all very much enhanced by leaders who are aware and compassionate—leaders who can embody and role-model the gift of being truly present with others. Rossi, whether in the kitchen or out in the fields on our farm, is always sensing what his people are experiencing. We are his flock and his role as shepherd is very deep and instinctual. He checks in with each of us regularly even while he's out looking for deer to chase. He always knows when there is stress or tension and will do his best to bring us back to an awareness of joy, love, and laughter in that very moment.

Each of us is a leader. We lead ourselves. We may lead families, teams, clubs, communities, or organizations of the largest imaginable size. And each of us needs to ask our version of "What would Rossi do?" each day.

Blair Morris

Each of us is a leader—we lead ourselves before we can effectively lead others. This is a principle that **BLAIR MORRIS** works with as a coach, consultant, meditation teacher, and facilitator. Blair founded Liminalities after a long career in healthcare and works with clients ready to be fully present and conscious in life and work. She lives with her family, dogs, and horses on a farm in the Mid-Atlantic.

TWENTY-FOUR

The Fall and Rise of General Lorna

Lorna Hagen

L eadership isn't just about making tough decisions or driving results. It's about inspiring, nurturing, and guiding others towards a shared vision. For years I thought I had it all figured out. I was a general in my own story, the woman with all the answers, the one people turned to when they needed solutions. "Madam Executive," as one of my leaders called me.

Little did I know, my command-and-control approach was setting me up for a soul-crushing reality check.

Despite my moniker, as a Chief People Officer—a title that simultaneously breeds respect and fear— for years I had consistently shown up with compassion for my teams, my leaders, and my companies.

There was Ellen, one of my direct reports, who faced an intense medical emergency at the height of the pandemic chaos. When she offered to bounce back after just a couple of days, I insisted she take all the time she needed before even considering returning to work. Her health and well-being came first, no questions asked.

Then there was the time when a miscommunication led to confusion about our team's role in producing a company-wide offsite. Instead of pointing fingers or reprimanding, I got on the phone with her to understand all the facts and collaboratively come up with solutions. I advocated for our team, never once playing the blame game.

In my start-up days, I remember moving my desk twice to sit right next to newly-hired seasoned corporate executives who were onboarding into these VC-backed private companies. I wanted to help them understand the dynamics and culture of smaller, younger, and more agile companies. It was about rolling up our sleeves together and relearning how to operate in a new environment.

And even during the painful process of layoffs, we strived to act with empathy. We were generous with severance, delayed exit dates to continue full parental leave, ensured each person got an individual meeting, and provided support throughout the transition. It was compassion in action.

Then in 2020 the world turned upside down. As the CPO of a billion-dollar company, I was tasked with driving a new, optimistic, and future-leaning vision for our ten thousand employees. The company had just emerged from financial distress and a lot was riding on our success. My job? Transform the culture, influence leadership, and reshape shareholder expectations. No pressure, right?

Three months into my role, COVID-19 hit. Suddenly we were grappling with deep cleaning protocols, return-to-work timelines, and mass communications to make employees feel safe when we often didn't know if we were right. Many of our employees were essential workers, and the weight of their safety and well-being pressed heavily on my shoulders.

In those early pandemic days I found myself leaning heavily into my General Lorna persona at work. I rallied my team, telling them that HR was finally in the big game and they needed to show up at 110 percent. I promised that eventually we'd get 110 percent back. And in many ways I did demonstrate compassionate leadership at work. Remember Ellen? And of course a round of furloughs that were hard on our employees and their families. But the true north was always, "How can we stay viable and help our employees through it?"

But while I was showing compassionate leadership at work, a different story was unfolding at home. My twin boys were failing school in the new remote learning environment. My approach? Tell them to work harder and do better. I wielded imaginary sticks (taking away video games and computers) instead of offering carrots (rewards for grades, helping around the house). The General was in full force, barking orders like a drill sergeant on steroids.

"I am the general, you are the soldiers," I'd tell my kids. As a single mom, solely responsible for their financial well-being, it was my way of keeping the chaos at bay, of feeling in control when life seemed determined to throw us curveballs. Little did I know, I was setting myself up for a reckoning that would make me question everything: my abilities, my beliefs, my competence. Hell, my entire identity was on the chopping block.

The disparity between my leadership at work and at home was stark. At work I was finding ways for my team to support each other, implementing rotations, encouraging staycations, and creating opportunities to refresh and recharge. At home I was being stoic and hard-hitting, and it wasn't working for anyone.

It was too much. Being General Mom at home was causing me to teeter on burnout in the most important job: guiding and growing my kids through a pandemic no one had ever experienced. I realized that my day job, everything I had always wanted, was diminishing my humanity at home. And I had to leave.

In a moment of desperation—or perhaps clarity—I ran away to Todos Santos, Mexico. I signed up for a retreat at the Modern Elder Academy which promised to help navigate transitions, specifically mid-life transitions. Because on top of everything else I was now embarking on my first job search in years, and doing it in middle age.

It was there, on a terrace overlooking the deep blue Pacific Ocean, that our guide posed a simple yet profound question. He asked us to think about a mindset we held. Without hesitation I thought of the phrase I often told my children: "I am the general, you are the soldiers."

"Now close your eyes," the guide instructed. "Does that mindset work for you?"

The tears came fast. In that moment I realized that General Lorna had taken over every aspect of my life. The tough exterior I had cultivated to navigate the corporate world and single parenthood had become a prison of my own making.

As I reflected on my journey I began to unravel my General mindset. It had its origins in this heightened sense of responsibility, always trying to have a "say-do ratio" of 100 percent. Later on, single parenthood and the weight of sole responsibility for three kids under the age of six compounded that need to always take care of everything. At work it manifested in high expectations and the unrelenting requests to constantly prove the value of the work I had chosen to do: human resources. While it had led to professional success, it came at a cost: a lack of self-compassion and missed opportunities for deeper collaboration and innovation.

The interconnection between my work identity and personal identity became glaringly apparent. I had allowed my professional persona to dictate my approach to parenting and had failed to recognize that different relationships require different leadership styles. How obtuse that I wasn't following the coaching I give all my leaders: "Meet your team where they are at, and communicate in ways that make sense to them." These three kids were getting the General instead of mom.

Rebuilding with compassion wasn't easy. It required vulnerability, a willingness to admit mistakes, and a commitment to change. At work I had already been implementing compassionate leadership practices. Now it was time to bring that same approach home.

I started by having open conversations with my kids about the pressures we were all facing. Instead of demanding perfection, we talked about effort and growth. I replaced the "general and soldiers" analogy with one of a team working together, each with our own strengths and challenges and needs. There were setbacks and moments of doubt. Old habits die hard, and there were times when General Lorna threatened to make a comeback. But with each stumble I reminded myself of the importance of self-compassion and the power of leading by example.

The positive outcomes were profound. My relationships at home improved dramatically. My daughter went off to college and finished a successful first year. My boys began to open up more, sharing alike their struggles and successes. We developed a more collaborative approach to problem-solving, whether it was tackling homework or navigating the challenges of driving, girls, and college applications.

This journey of compassionate leadership is ongoing. It's about continuous learning and growth, about balancing compassion for others with self-compassion. It's about recognizing that true strength lies not in unyielding authority, but in the ability to adapt, empathize, and inspire.

As I look back on this transformation, I'm struck by the broader implications for leadership in both professional and personal contexts. The job will never love you, hold you, or comfort you. It's crucial to be intentional about what or who is most important in your life. Are you giving them 100 percent and expecting very little in return? Are you allowing yourself to be vulnerable?

Most importantly, are you acting as a beacon of true north in action and words for your teams—both personal and professional? Compassionate leadership isn't about being soft or lowering standards. It's about recognizing the humanity in ourselves and others, about creating environments where people can thrive and not just survive.

To cultivate compassionate leadership, consider these three key strategies:

1. **Practice compassion in action.** Remove roadblocks for your team. Actively identify and eliminate obstacles that hinder your team's progress. This might mean streamlining processes, advocating for resources, or even challenging organizational norms. When you clear the path for your team, you demonstrate by your actions that their success is your priority.

2. **Practice active listening.** Truly hear what others are saying, not just with your ears but with your heart. This means setting aside your own agenda and fully focusing on understanding the other person's perspective. Use this insight to inform your actions and decisions.

3. **Lead by example.** Show vulnerability, admit mistakes, and demonstrate the behaviors you want to see in others. Compassionate leadership isn't about perfection; it's about authenticity and continuous growth. When you model compassion, you create a culture where it can flourish.

As you embark on your own journey towards compassionate leadership, remember that it's not about being soft or lowering standards. It's about recognizing the humanity in ourselves and others, about creating environments where people can thrive, not just survive. This approach has the power to transform not just your professional life, but your personal relationships as well.

In the end, the most profound lesson I learned was that compassionate leadership is as much about doing as it is about being. It's about taking concrete steps to support your team, to foster growth, and to create a positive environment. The fall of General Lorna led to the rise of a more authentic and compassionate leader —one who understands that true strength lies in empathy, action, and the courage to change. As you navigate your own leadership path I challenge you to find that balance between driving results and nurturing growth. The impact you can have, both in your workplace and at home, is immeasurable. Remember: compassionate leadership isn't just a mindset. It's a practice that requires consistent effort and tangible actions.

Lorna Hagen

LORNA HAGEN is a Human Capital leader, Executive Coach, and co-founder of WIN Consulting, drawing from her twenty-plus years of experience as a Chief People Officer at companies including iHeart Media, Guild Education, and OnDeck Capital. Her passion lies in teaching leaders to balance driving results while cultivating compassionate leadership. With her three kids soon heading to college, Lorna is excited to embrace her empty 'nexting' chapter through ballroom dancing and world exploration - all while continuing to champion equitable opportunities for all.

TWENTY-FIVE

Biking with My Amygdala

Scott Shute

I was cycling with a friend in the Santa Cruz mountains in the San Francisco Bay area. We had just climbed up the famous (for local bikers) Old LaHonda Road, a test of grit and endurance but also breathtaking. The road curves and heaves through old-growth redwoods. On this Sunday morning it felt like church, otherworldly light streaming in between the misty branches.

We were on a connecting highway to our next redwood adventure, climbing around a long curve, catching up on busy lives. There was no shoulder on this highway, and because of the traffic patterns, cars had to slow down to pass us.

I was jolted out of my Sunday-morning cocoon by a young man shouting, his fury directed at me. Apparently, slowing down for twelve seconds triggered something primal. It was war. A black cloud of hate descended on us all.

His torso was all the way out of the pickup truck's passenger window. Foaming at the mouth, fangs bared, he proceeded to scream every nasty insult, every disgusting name he could think of, in the six seconds it took to drive away.

My nervous system went tilt. I was ready for battle. But here among my redwood sanctuary, I had started from a place of deep peace so I didn't succumb to the fight. I shouted back to him, as neutrally as I could muster.

"Hey, you have a great day!" I tried to mean it.

Thankfully he and his buddy didn't do a U-turn to deepen the conversation.

I was proud of my external response. It could have gone worse. The black cloud followed the young man away, leaving me in Sunday sunshine. But on the inside I was shaken. Our interaction left a stain on my heart.

As a biker, it's a strange vulnerability, navigating a sixteen-pound bike amongst three-thousand-pound cars, protected by a thin (and admittedly dorky) layer of spandex. There's a lot of trust required.

More recently, I was biking in my neighborhood, returning from a long ride with my son, Kam. We've been riding together in some form or another since he was a toddler. Now he's a fully-launched adult and I'm the one struggling to keep up.

A car full of twenty-somethings passed and a young guy leaned out the window and shouted at me. He pulled himself back into the car and I could hear them all laughing. My eyes narrowed. The stain in my heart was trying to return, to separate me from my goodwill—to separate me from this young man. I prepared for battle.

We were on surface streets and I could tell that his car would be stopped ahead of me at the next light. There would be opportunity for more interaction. I hadn't heard what he had shouted. I assumed the worst. I was considering several choice responses, or perhaps a hand gesture.

I slowed as I rolled past his car on the way to meet my son at the light, two feet away from the young man through his open car window.

"What did you say?"

I aimed for neutrality, my nervous system shaking inside, primed for conflict—bracing myself for his anger. For his hate. For the black cloud to descend upon us all.

He smiled a huge goofy smile and as I rode past he said, "What's your FTP?"

I slowed to a stop next to Kam and asked him, "What's FTP again?"

"Functional Threshold Power," he replied calmly, unaware of the action that was taking place behind him.

I softened, shook my head, and smiled. FTP is a nerdy, super-specific measure of how much power a cyclist can hold for a certain amount of time. It's essentially a measure of how strong of a rider you are.

This guy was from my tribe! There was no threat. He was just a goofy labrador retriever, leaning out the window, barking at the other dogs, happy to be alive, celebrating in the wonder of the sunshine.

Now that I was in on the joke I called back to him, "300!"

"Really?!!" His eyes got big.

If my FTP is 300 I am a biking god. I am a legend. He is in the presence of greatness. He might want to hop out and get my autograph. Ha! The real truth is a number *much* less than that.

I laughed and shook my head "No!"—my eyes glowing with connection. More laughter. I have been this kid. I have shouted silly things at strangers while in the presence of my teenage crew, looking for a laugh while cruising. In my darkest moments I have probably shouted worse, like the guy raging on Old LaHonda Road. If I haven't, I've thought it.

As we rode away my quiet took over. How often? How often do I make this assumption about people? About situations? How often does my nervous system assume the worst and prepare for battle, only to relax again and again and again in the face of non-danger.

Yes, sometimes the threat is real, and I'm grateful for my over-active amygdala and the nervous system that keeps me alive. But most of the time—not so much.

I'm reminded of something wise attributed to Mark Twain: "I've lived through a lot of terrible things in my time, some of which actually happened."

How often does this happen to us?

We are experts in picking up signals from others. Our bodies, emotions, and intuitions are finely tuned to look for clues from others about meaning.

Sadly, we're often wrong.

This fine-tuning is very much influenced by our amygdala—our survival response. The amygdala is constantly scanning our lives for danger. As we were evolving over the last few hundred thousand years, our bodies and minds developed to be highly sensitive to anything that might kill us. In the old days, maybe it was the sound of a predator walking in the tall grass or the scent of a neighboring tribe's fire. These days our nervous systems might get triggered by an angry email, a careless driver, or the sarcastic wit of someone we don't know very well.

You've probably heard the term "Fight, Flight, or Freeze" to describe these very deeply programmed instincts. Our reactions to many situations, regardless of the actual level of danger involved, are nearly always rooted in this primal survival mechanism. In short, we view the world as way more dangerous and negative than it actually is.

That is a fantastic strategy for staying alive. It's often a problem for developing compassion.

The meaning we attribute to others' actions is shaded toward survival. This means that we often assume the very worst from what someone said.

We get a performance review and, along with the five pages of amazing feedback on what we've done well, there are three sentences about the things we could do better next time. We obsess about these three sentences and somehow end up in a negative thought train that leads to worrying about losing our jobs.

Survival.

We have an argument with our partner. We are hurt by what they say and our negative thought train leads us to worrying about them leaving us and our being alone.

Survival.

We have a cordial discussion with a neighbor about the fence that separates our properties. We start thinking about a prior neighbor who caused a stink about our fence and created strain on that relationship. Our negative thoughts cloud this relationship with the new neighbor, leading us to assume that they will eventually start acting like the old neighbor and are not to be trusted. We think this worry will keep us safe.

Survival.

This survival response keeps us separated from our true nature. It keeps us separated from each other. While we (sometimes!) give our love to those who are close and have earned our trust, we often keep others at arm's length, assuming the worst from them so we'll stay safe.

The biggest blocker of compassion towards others is our own fearful patterns.

Moving from fear (survival) to love (compassion) starts from the inside out. Here are three things that can help:

Recognizing our triggers: self-awareness. So many things set us off. When we're really upset our ability to think rationally and to operate from a place of abundance and grace is thrown out the window.

When we're upset, instead of focusing on the other person, we can notice that we've been triggered and ask ourselves, "What is still developing within me that allows this interaction to throw me off balance?"

Using my example of the guy in the pickup truck screaming at me, first, there was actual danger. He could have pulled over and gotten violent, so my amygdala was correct to be on edge. But there was something more. He was screaming names at me that no one has called me since I was a teenager. When I was younger these names cut deeply and caused me to feel terribly about myself. They caused a real separation from my peers.

Survival.

Now as an adult, I'm comfortable with my friend group. I'm comfortable in my own skin.

When triggered, we can assess the situation logically. Am I in real danger? What's the worst that can happen? Is that likely? What am I really upset about? Does that really have anything to do with this situation?

Comforting the amygdala: self-compassion. The amygdala response is one of the many voices in our heads competing for attention. It gives us a constant stream of information about what's wrong or dangerous. It's important to counterbalance those thoughts. Think of them as affirmations. Here are a few that I find powerful and effective:

"I am safe."

"I am fine. Relax."

"I have everything I need."

Create some of your own that feel right for you. Those will likely be the most powerful and effective.

Curiosity and understanding: compassion. True compassion starts with curiosity. Having an understanding, an awareness of the other person. Yes, it's hard to be curious when someone is screaming at you or you feel like you're under attack.

I thought about the young man in the pickup truck. Have I ever been in a hurry, and someone caused me a delay? Yes, I know what that feels like.

Have I ever been frustrated with someone who is different than me and screamed at them? Ok, maybe not since junior high, but I'm sure I've wanted to!

Have I ever been annoyed with my own life so much so that any provocation caused my already frustrated self to get even more out of control. Yes. I can understand that. I definitely experienced that emotion when I was a teenager. Just like him.

When we move from judgement to recognition, we can *start* to see ourselves in another person.

When we can see the best in ourselves, we can *start* to see the best in others.

When we see the best in others, we can *start* to treat both ourselves and others with unconditional love.

And *that*, for me, is worth the effort to quiet that ever-present survival instinct.

Scott Shute

Scott Shute's mission is to change work from the inside out. He blends his experience as a Silicon Valley executive (LinkedIn) with his lifelong practice and passion as a wisdom-seeker and teacher. He is the author of the award-winning book *The Full Body Yes*.

Notes

The Courage In Compassion

1. Einstein, Albert. "The Einstein Papers. A Man of Many Parts." *New York Times*, March 29 (1972): 1.

The Grace in Change

1. Campbell, Joseph. *Pathways to Bliss: Mythology and Personal Transformation*. New World Library (2004): 129.

7. Slowing Down and Showing Up

1. Pride inside at Intel: Why Accurate Pronouns and Inclusive Language Are So Important." *Intel Community*, 9 June 2021, community.intel.-com/t5/Blogs/Intel/We-Are-Intel/Pride-Inside-at-Intel-Why-Accurate-Pronouns-and-Inclusive/post/1334612.
2. "Intel 2021-22 Corporate Responsibility Report." Intel, 2022. csrreportbuilder.intel.com/pdfbuilder/pdfs/CSR-2021-22-Full-Report.pdf.

8. Use of Self

1. Jamieson, David W., Matthew Auron, and David Shechtman. "Managing use of self for masterful professional practice." *Organization Development Practitioner* (2010): 42(3),1-11.
2. Culbert, S. "The interpersonal process of self-disclosure: It takes two to know one." *New Directions In Client-Centered Therapy*. Houghton Mifflin, 1967).

9. Itchy Bumps

1. Kabat-Zinn, Jon, *Full Catastrophe Living: Using the wisdom of your body and mind to face stress, pain, and illness*. Delta, 2009.
2. McGonigal, Kelly. *The Upside of Stress: Why Stress Is Good for You, and How to Get Good at It*. Avery, 2016.

The Power in Empathy

1. Kabat-Zinn, Jon. *Mindfulness Meditation For Everyday Life.* Piatkus (2001): 92.

13. Lights! Camera! Engagement!

1. McCraty, Rollin. *Science of the Heart.* Vol 2. Movement Publishing, 2015.
2. McCraty, Rollin and Maria A Zayass. "Cardiac coherence, self-regulation, autonomic stability, and psychosocial well-being." *Frontiers in Psychology* 5 (2014), 1090.
3. Neilson, Kate and Heath Dunn. "Infographic: How we spend our time at work." *Australian HR Institute.* December (2023).
4. Hougaard, Rasmus, Carter, Jacqueline, and Louise Chester. "Power Can Corrupt Leaders, Compassion Can Save Them." *Harvard Business Review*, February (2018); Worline, Monica C. and Jane E. Dutton. *Awakening Compassion at Work.* Berrett Koehler, 2017.

14. All Rise

1. "A Heartfelt Tribute to Our Founder on His 103rd Birthday." Chick-fil-A, 24 Mar. 2024, www.chick-fil-a.com/press-room/a-heartfelt-tribute-to-our-founder-on-his-103rd-birthday. Press release.

The Purpose in Witnessing

1. Maté, Gabor. *When The Body Says No: The Cost Of Hidden Stress.* Vintage Canada, 2011.

18. Seeing Deeply

1. Hickstead, Jessica Lynne. *Stigma Associated with Invisible Disabilities and Its Effect on Intended Disclosure in the Workplace.* Walden University Dissertations and Doctoral Studies Collection, 2023.

The Strength in Conscious Awareness

1. Brown, Brené. *Atlas of the Heart: Mapping Meaningful Connection and the Language Of Human Experience.* Random House (2021): 117.

About Changing Work

Changing Work is a movement deeply committed to revolutionizing the dynamics of the workplace from within.

Our Vision is to **Change Work from the Inside Out.**

Essentially, we are here to make work a more humane, conscious, and nurturing environment; an experience that promotes personal growth, self-awareness, and compassion, while continuing to deliver value to all stakeholders. We recognize that profitability is important, and that it comes with a need for balance not only for shareholders but also for employees, customers, and the broader global community—a world that works for everyone.

Changing Work is a collective of business leaders, employees, coaches, and consultants. Fundamentally, we do two things:

First, we build community. There's something incredibly powerful about being on a journey together with people who are bonded by a desire for a common good. One of our favorite things is our monthly community meeting. There's so much love in the room!

Second, we share best practices. This comes in many forms, including the book in your hands right now. We also have a podcast, a newsletter, courses, cohort-based learning, and so much more.

Have something you'd like to share? Or something you'd like to learn? Or would you just like to be surrounded by like-hearted people?

Come join us at **www.changingwork.org**

www.ingramcontent.com/pod-product-compliance
Lightning Source LLC
Chambersburg PA
CBHW060804120626

46557CB00001B/78